THE BRIGHTON BELLE

STEPHEN GRANT AND SIMON JEFFS

Capital Transport

ACKNOWLEDGEMENTS

The authors would like to thank all the photographers, Pullman enthusiasts and organisations for providing material for this book. Special thanks go to John Scrace, Clinton Shaw, Michael Baker and for providing many of the wonderful photos, Antony Ford for making available some of his precious collection of Belle artefacts to photograph and scan, Denis Dunstone and Neil Marshall of the Transport Trust and all the supporters of the 5 BEL Project for their visionary scheme to bring the Belle back, and the staff of the Bluebell Railway. We would also like to thank the many people who contributed factual material, anecdotes and pictures to the book and to salute the small but dedicated band of enthusiasts who are working hard to restore Southern Electric trains to operating condition. Special thanks go to Michael Welch for his assistance with correcting some of the text for this second edition and for researching most of the additional photographs. He was assisted in his task by John Atkinson, John Beckett, Graham Burtenshaw, Mike Cruttenden, Chris Evans, Dave Fakes, David Jones, Charles Long, Roger Merry-Price and David Wigley. Thanks, too, to our wives for their tolerance of our attention over a long period of time to Audrey, Doris, Gwen, Hazel, Mona, Vera and the other Brighton Belles.

The 'Brighton Belle' arch over the entrance to Platform 17 at Victoria station in the 1960s. *Transport Trust Collection*

First published 2011
Second edition 2012

ISBN 978-185414-362-4

Published by Capital Transport Publishing Ltd
www.capitaltransport.com

Printed by 1010 Printing International Ltd

Contents

Title page Comfortable, cosy, intimate and opulent. The Brighton Belle was a train with style and character in abundance; it was like a 'souvenir' of the railway's golden age. Here, at Victoria on 27th April 1972, shortly before the train's demise, patrons have already taken their seats prior to the train's departure to Brighton at 19.00. *Chris Evans*

Back cover The 11.00am Victoria to Brighton train, with unit No.3053 leading, approaches Merstham on 7th October 1962, a day when the Quarry Line was closed due to engineering work and services diverted to run via Redhill. The photographer is standing on the trackbed of a former industrial branch which served Peter's lime siding. *John Beckett*

Chapter 1
Beginnings

Brighton had been a fishing town in decline until, in the 18th century, Dr Richard Russell pronounced that drinking and bathing in sea-water could cure an astonishingly wide variety of illnesses, ranging from constipation and 'fluxions' to incipient insanity.

King George III took the waters at Weymouth, though with no obvious benefit to that unfortunate monarch's state of health. His son, the Prince of Wales and the future George IV, made frequent trips to Brighton to bathe and to pursue his gambling, drinking and amorous affairs out of sight of his censorious father. He adapted and extended a seafront farmhouse to become his neo-classical Marine Pavilion and later commissioned the architect John Nash to further extend and rebuild this pleasure-dome into the exotic Royal Pavilion that still stands today as one of Brighton's principal visitor attractions.

Royal patronage made Brighton a fashionable resort – close enough to London for the journey by coach not to be too daunting but far enough away to maintain exclusivity. Wealthy visitors could dance and play cards in spacious new Assembly Rooms. Areas to the east and the west of the original town were developed in elegant style and a chain pier was built from which, for a time, a steamship operated to France. The new watering-place made an impression on society – Jane Austen alluded to it in a novel that she was writing just before she died in 1817.

Meanwhile, in the less genteel surroundings of the Cornish tin mines, Richard Trevithick was finding out how to apply the steam force of Newcomen and Watt's ponderous, stationary beam engines in a high-pressure mobile power-pack. In 1804 he demonstrated a practical steam locomotive and the idea was taken forward by others, notably George Stephenson. The Stockton and Darlington railway opened for traffic in 1825 with a mix of steam and horse power, followed in 1831 by the world's first inter-city passenger and freight steam railway, from Liverpool to Manchester. Fuelled by the Industrial Revolution's pent-up demand for low-cost transport and by *laissez-faire* capitalism at its most uninhibited, Britain's railway network grew at an explosive rate.

The railway reached Brighton from London Bridge in September 1841. It was a superbly engineered line, with John Rastrick's beautiful viaduct over the River Ouse and three long tunnels at Merstham, Balcombe and Clayton, the last with a castellated portal at the northern entrance. The route of the future 'Brighton Belle', from Victoria rather than London Bridge, was not completed until 1862. At Brighton, the architect David Mocatta designed an Italianate station frontage to be complemented from 1882 by a beautifully-proportioned train shed that followed the curved alignment of the platforms.

As early as 1844, the London and Brighton Railway was offering First Class season tickets from Brighton to London Bridge at £50 *per annum*. To cater for this market the company laid on an all-First Class express, the forerunner of the future 'City Limited', which left Brighton at 8.45am and made the journey to London Bridge in 90 minutes. The return working left London Bridge at 4.40pm and reached Brighton at 6.15pm. Already Brighton was within commuting distance of London. The LBSCR also encouraged day trippers to Brighton, the regular service being supplemented during the summer by briskly-timed excursion trains made up of open-sided Third Class carriages. The railway had strengthened and expanded the economic and social association between the capital and this raffishly-elegant resort and this in turn created more demand for high-quality passenger services.

Opposite: The Brighton Terminus of the London & Brighton Railway, c 1845. Designed by David Mocatta the station was built high on the western slope of the valley through which the road from London enters the town. *NRM/Science & Society Picture Library*

Meanwhile, in America, the railroad network was also growing rapidly. George Mortimer Pullman worked for his brother's cabinet-making firm, where he developed an appreciation both of fine craftsmanship and of the rigours of long distance railroad travel. Perceiving a market for something better than the spartan passenger saloons of the North American railroads of the day, Pullman developed and refined the concept of the sleeping car. By the 1860s he had placed fleets of cars, built in his own works, with several North American long-distance railroads which hauled them in their own trains and maintained the running gear. Pullman passengers paid the basic fare to the railroad and a supplement to the Pullman company for the enhanced comfort of these convertible day/sleeping cars and for the services of an attendant.

In 19th century America, as in Britain, long-distance trains used to make brief stops to enable passengers to bolt a hasty meal at the station refreshment room. With their captive markets these, and by association railway catering in general, became a byword for poor quality food and service. Mindful of this, Pullman built their first 'Hotel Car' in 1867, being a convertible day/sleeper with kitchen where a chef would prepare food for the occupants during the journey. At mealtimes, the attendant would put up tables between the seats and set them with linen tablecloths and fine crockery and cutlery.

From this, it was a logical step to providing dining cars, available to all passengers on a day train.

Under its General Manager James Allport, Britain's Midland Railway was also developing a reputation for comfort. Allport was familiar with Pullman's operations in America and in 1873 Pullman contracted with the Midland to supply 16 cars for its main-line services. These were a mix of convertible day/sleeping cars for Anglo-Scottish routes and 'Parlour Cars' for shorter-distance journeys. Built in the Pullman Standard factory in Detroit and re-assembled in Pullman's own works at Derby, these cars closely followed contemporary American practice with a large saloon body mounted on bogies and with open verandas at each end. However the British public, or at least that part of it that could afford a First Class fare and a supplement, was initially slow to warm to the saloon format, with many preferring the semi-privacy of a compartment. From an operating point of view, the Pullman cars were heavy, about twice the weight per passenger of a contemporary British compartment vehicle. These were serious disadvantages given the relatively small locomotives and light track of the time, and the Midland eventually phased out its Pullman operations in favour of providing its own sleeping and restaurant cars. It did, however, purchase the Pullman cars and take them into its own stock.

Chapter 2
Brighton Line Pullmans

The LBSCR always was rather superior. In Oscar Wilde's 1895 play, 'The Importance of Being Ernest', Jack admits to having been left as a baby in a handbag at London's Victoria station adding, by way of mitigation, 'the Brighton line'. As Hamilton Ellis points out[1], when Lady Bracknell retorts 'the line is immaterial' she is quite wrong – an inferior foundling would have been discovered on the Chatham line's adjacent premises.

In 1875, the Pullman company approached the LBSCR Board with a proposal to operate a Pullman car between Victoria and Brighton. Newly-built 'Mars' was chosen and was operated on the LBSCR as a parlour car. This experiment must have been a success because three more cars – 'Alexandra', 'Albert Edward' and 'Globe' were added to the LBSCR-hauled fleet over the next couple of years.

Given the origins of the Pullman brand as a comfortable means of long-distance travel, it is perhaps surprising that the company should come to be associated for almost a century with the Brighton line, one of the shortest main lines in Britain. Yet one can see how it came to succeed so well here. The LBSCR had already developed a market for commuting between an office in the smoky city and a family home in the healthy air of the Sussex coast. For these wealthy gentlemen commuters, the Pullman Parlour Cars had something of the ambience of a London club. Ladies travelling alone found the open layout and the presence of an attendant more secure and reassuring than a compartment in a non-corridor carriage. And for pleasure seekers, perhaps looking to impress their travelling companions, a Pullman car had style.

Pleased with the commercial success of the individual Parlour Cars, Pullman and the LBSCR launched their first all-Pullman express in 1881, operating between London and Brighton twice daily in each direction. Sunday patronage, however, proved to be so light that the service on this day was withdrawn after a short period. The train was made up of four cars, named 'Beatrice', 'Louise', 'Maud' and 'Victoria' in honour of children of the Royal family. 'Beatrice' was the

former 'Globe' and the other three cars were re-named transfers from the Midland line. Though not new, the refurbished cars had several innovations. 'Victoria' incorporated a small pantry buffet for the service of tea and sandwiches and the four cars were heated by oil-fired hot water systems – previously the best the winter traveller could hope for was a pre-heated foot-warmer. Perhaps most significantly in view of later developments, the train was lit by electricity. Edison lamps were powered by Fauré accumulator cells pre-charged by a steam-driven dynamo at Victoria and sufficient for six hours of operation.

The inaugural run of this 'Pullman Limited Express' took place on Monday 5th December 1881 following two press and promotional trips the week before. A contemporary reporter wrote: 'At all the stations at which the train stopped, persons on the platform were struck with the novelty of this "moveable hotel." Few of the saloons of the great ocean going steamers excel the excellence of the arrangements in the Brighton Limited Pullman Car train'.

In 1888, the Pullman Company Ltd (a wholly-owned subsidiary of Pullman's Palace Car Company in the US), ordered three all-new cars from the American parent's Illinois factory specifically for the Brighton line. Shipped in 'knocked down'

Interior of the parlour car 'Her Majesty' from the three-car 1895 Pullman set. *Charles Long Collection*

---

1 Hamilton Ellis, C. 'The London Brighton and South Coast Railway' London: Ian Allan, 1960, p11.

form, these were assembled by the LBSCR at their Brighton works (the Pullman Company's own workshop at Preston Park was to come later). These cars, 'Prince', 'Princess' and 'Albert Victor', incorporated several further developments. Like the 1881 set they were fitted with the Westinghouse automatic air brake, a system that the LBSCR was in process of adopting as a standard for all of its passenger fleet. The three were semi-permanently coupled together by means of bar couplings and what was to become known as the Pullman gangway – a sprung vertical end-frame that both provided a safe passage from one car to the next and acted as a buffer to absorb shocks and reduce swaying. Like the 1881 train, these cars were lit by electricity but, following successful experiments by William Stroudley, the LBSCR's Chief Mechanical Engineer of the day, the power source was now a dynamo turned by an axle-driven belt. The dynamo was mounted in the so-called 'Pullman Pup', a guard's and luggage van supplied by the LBSCR but styled and painted to match the Pullman cars.

This set was followed in 1895 by three more cars, 'Her Majesty', 'Duchess of York' and 'Princess of Wales' together with an accompanying Pup, thus providing two complete sets for Brighton line services, although in practice these sets often operated in trains that also included non-Pullman LBSCR stock. The earlier cars, suitably updated, also continued in service and often operated singly on LBSCR services to Brighton, Eastbourne and Hastings or on boat trains to Newhaven that connected with cross-channel steamers to France.

In 1898 the LBSCR re-launched its Sunday Pullman service to Brighton, originally as the 'Sunday Pullman Limited' but soon renamed the 'Brighton Limited'. This was a genuinely all-Pullman train, First Class only plus supplement. Pullman cars 'Her Majesty', 'Duchess of York' and 'Princess of Wales' were paired with the earlier 'Beatrice' and 'Victoria' and flanked by the two Pups. Hauled by No. 206 'Smeaton', one of the LBSCR's elegant new Class B2 4-4-0 express locomotives designed by Robert Billinton, the inaugural run was completed in just 60 minutes. This was the Naughty Nineties, the era of Aubrey Beardsley's beautifully decadent artwork and Oscar Wilde's wittily amoral plays, whilst the rigid social structures of the high-Victorian era were being challenged by the first stirrings of the suffragette movement. The new Sunday service was an instant success.

Though it had so far failed to prosper on the other British main lines, Pullman was going from strength to strength on the LBSCR, so much so that more new cars were quickly ordered. 'The Arundel' and 'The Chichester' (1899), 'Devonshire' (1900), 'Duchess of Norfolk', 'Princess Ena' and 'Princess Patricia' (all 1906) were the last Pullmans to be supplied from the Illinois factory and the last with clerestory roofs, but in many ways they were the prototypes of the classic British Pullman car of the 20th century. Mounted on tri-axle bogies and with 64ft long bodies, these impressive cars had large, rectangular windows, pivoted revolving armchairs and electric lighting.

Such was the close relationship between the LBSCR and Pullman that the 1906 cars adopted a new livery of umber brown – a shade that matched the LBSCR's latest livery – and ivory white upper panels. With the later addition of an umber strip at cantrail level, this was to be the standard livery for all British Pullmans until the mid 1960s.

The first all-Pullman service between Victoria and Brighton is seen at Brighton after its inaugural public journey on Monday 5th December 1881. The locomotive is the London Brighton and South Coast Railway's Stroudley Class G 2-2-2 No. 334, 'Petworth'. Note that the coal in the tender has been whitewashed – then a common practice for royal and other special workings. The Pullman cars were named Maud, Victoria, Beatrice and Louise. This was the first train in the world to be equipped throughout with electric lighting, which was powered by accumulators in the baggage compartments in the end vehicles. *Charles Long Collection*

Chapter 3
The Southern Belle

Mr Davison Dalziel, financier, and later *President du Conseil* of the *Compagnie Internationale des Wagons-Lits* (from 1919), successfully acquired Pullman's UK business in 1907. He bought it through his own company, Drawing Room Cars, and floated it in 1915 as the Pullman Car Co. Ltd. Dalziel brought new energy to a business that had previously been peripheral to Pullman's North American empire, his strategy being to build on the success of the LBSCR operations as a basis for expansion within Britain. As a first step, he awarded a contract to the Birmingham-based Metropolitan Amalgamated Carriage and Wagon Co. Ltd to construct seven sumptuous new 12-wheel cars to operate the Southern Belle, a new daily all-Pullman express service to Brighton.

The new cars were a further development of the 1899-1906 build, less obviously American in appearance as they had a plain, elliptical roof in place of the former clerestory. Each car was 63ft 10ins long, 8ft 8¾ins wide and 13ft 2ins high. The two end cars, 'Verona' and 'Alberta' included a guard's compartment with room for luggage. Electricity was supplied from underfloor accumulators on each car, charged by axle-driven dynamos. By 1912, the cars were heated by a supply of low-pressure steam from the locomotive, in line with emerging standard practice on UK railways. Like the earlier US-built cars, they also had two-piece lifting sash windows with decorative leaded panes in the upper sections as well as a supply of warmed, filtered fresh air through ventilator ducts.

LBSCR Class H1 4-4-2 No. 41 at Victoria with the Southern Belle. The painting is by 'F Moore', the collective name of a studio of artists operating in the first two decades of the 20th century who produced many paintings and painted photographs of steam locomotives prior to the advent of colour photography. *NRM/Science & Society Picture Library*

Interior of the 1908 Southern Belle car 'Belgravia', taken from the Southern Belle publicity brochure. Like their US-built predecessors, the 1908 cars initially had solid-fuel Baker stoves heating circulating hot water. They were not equipped with steam heating until 1912. The leaded panes in the upper sections of the sash windows were simply decorative, not opening ventilators.

LBSCR Class H2 4-4-2 locomotive 422 departs from Victoria station with the Southern Belle. The locomotive carries the LBSCR's umber brown livery, matched by the umber and cream of the 1908 Pullman cars. No. 422 entered service in July 1911 and remained in traffic until October 1956, so it had a very good innings. The overhead current supply equipment for the LBSCR's suburban electric services can be seen to the right of the picture. *Bluebell Railway Museum*

Internally, the cars were furnished in three different decorative styles. The 'Verona' and 'Alberta' were described as 'French Renaissance', the 'Princess Helen', 'Grosvenor' and 'Bessborough' were finished in the Adam style and the 'Belgravia' and 'Cleopatra' were based on the 18th century decorative work of Michelangelo Pergolesi. 'Grosvenor' included a central kitchen and pantry from which stewards collected meals, sandwiches, beverages, etc., to be served to customers at their seats throughout the train. It also had a small transverse bar for the sale of items such as cigars.

The Southern Belle, which Dalziel claimed to be the 'world's most luxurious train', was launched on 1st November 1908 with a fanfare of publicity. A brochure gushed: '*Upon entering the Southern Belle we leave London behind … we have come to a place of enchantment, of beauty and exquisite comfort there are many cosy corners where two young people may sit at ease in a snug way and say to each other those vastly important things which belong to the philosophy of youth and love … the girl pretty and charmingly dressed and with very bright eyes, the man smart and well-groomed … as the train speeds on its way the sun shines through the window upon them, bathing them in a golden glamour … but old or young, tired or full of health and vigour, all are at their ease and delighted with this train which provides every conceivable luxury and is exquisite in its artistic decoration*'. The brochure concluded on a more mercenary note: '*all these advantages of a swift and delightful journey may be obtained for 12 shillings, the cost of a return ticket*'.

So successful was the Southern Belle that it was soon making two return trips to Brighton each day, three on Sundays. A further two similar cars, 'Vivienne' and 'Myrtle', the latter described as a buffet car, were added in 1911 to help cope with peak demand. The LBSCR had no restaurant or buffet cars of its own so Pullman cars, individually or in pairs, provided on-board catering on many of the company's other principal services between London and the coast. From 1908, four of the older cars operated the 'Eastbourne Pullman Limited', a Sunday-only all-Pullman service.

Since 1913, Third Class ordinary carriages had been added to nominally all-Pullman services and in 1915 the company took the decisive step of offering Third Class Pullmans. These were older cars, re-configured with 2+2 in fixed seating in four-seat bays on one side of an aisle and two-seat bays on the other in place of the 1+1 loose armchairs of the First Class fleet. Apart from this slight reduction in comfort, the Third Class cars were every bit as Pullman as the others, both in style and in service, and a huge improvement on the LBSCR's rather basic provision for the thrifty.

The railways had been placed under Government control from 1914 to support the war effort and by 1918 some were in a weak financial state, facing backlogs of asset maintenance and renewals, staff shortages and sharp increases in costs. The Government seriously considered nationalisation but the eventual decision, enshrined in the 1921 Railways Act, was compulsory grouping of 120 pre-1914 railway companies into four systems with effect from 1st January 1923. The LBSCR and its neighbours were amalgamated into the Southern Railway, an empire that extended from Broadstairs and Ramsgate in the east to Padstow in the west.

The Southern Railway was fortunate in having the dynamic and charismatic Sir Herbert Walker as its General Manager. He had been General Manager of the London and South Western Railway (LSWR) and had been deputy head of the wartime Railway Executive Committee, reporting to the Government. Walker lost no time in welding the Southern's disparate constituent companies into a strong, forward-thinking and customer-focused business. Walker took a pragmatic view of on-board catering arrangements. On-train catering on the former LBSCR and South Eastern routes had been provided by the Pullman company and these arrangements were confirmed and extended. On the other hand, hoteliers Spiers and Pond had run the LSWR's restaurant and pantry cars, evidently to Walker's satisfaction as the Southern renewed their contract for its South Western division and for all of its inter-regional services.

The 1920s were a period of steady expansion for the Pullman Car Company, which had now established a second stronghold on the London and North Eastern Railway as well as its smaller operations in Scotland and even on the Metropolitan Railway. The Southern Railway laid on a new all-Pullman boat train to Dover that became the 'Golden Arrow' in 1926, when the French Nord company inaugurated a matching luxury service from Calais to Paris. By then, some 60 Pullman cars were operating on the Southern's Sussex coast routes to Brighton, Worthing, Eastbourne, Newhaven and Hastings.

The Southern Railway announced that an 'entirely new' Southern Belle train would enter service on 1st January 1925 though 'new' merely meant 'different', with a mix of Third Class cars rebuilt from Great War ambulance train stock and First Class cars sourced from stock originally intended for LNER or Southern Railway Eastern Section routes. These included 'Iolanthe', 'Viking' and 'Rosamund', supplemented as required by cars from the 1908 train and even the earlier American cars.

Class H1 4-4-2 'Atlantic' No. 39, designed and built by the LBSCR under the supervision of its Chief Mechanical Engineer, Douglas Earle Marsh, had hauled the 'Southern Belle' on its inaugural run in 1908 and class H1 and H2 Atlantics continued to be used on the service right up to the end of steam haulage, seeming to have no difficulty keeping schedule. From 1914 onwards these Atlantics were supplemented by Lawson Billinton's large, fast and powerful 4-6-4 'Baltic' tank locomotives of class L and from 1926 by the Southern Railway's new 'King Arthur' class 4-6-0s, with their romantic, if historically dubious, names of knights of the Round Table.

In 1928 the Pullman Car Company leased part of the former LBSCR's workshops and stores at Preston Park, a mile or so north of Brighton station. Here the Company's craftsmen would overhaul, and even on occasion completely rebuild, Pullman cars from all parts of the UK.

LBSCR Class H2 4-4-2 locomotive 424, built in 1911, with a Southern Belle service made up of five of the 1908-1911 Pullman cars. The Pullman Company painted the roofs of their cars white but these quickly weathered to dark grey in the sooty conditions of a steam railway. The roof of the second car, still-white, suggests that it is 'Vivienne' or 'Myrtle', built in 1911 to supplement the original seven cars in response to the commercial success of the new service. No. 424 was designed by D. Earle Marsh and was based on the Ivatt 'Atlantics' of the Great Northern Railway. Named *Beachy Head* by the Southern Railway she had a long and successful career, continuing in service until 1958. *Mike Morant collection*

The luxury of Pullman as represented in this enticing scene, with the smartly dressed attendant about to enter the saloon with a tray of drinks. Its elegantly dressed passengers relax during the hour long journey from London to Brighton.

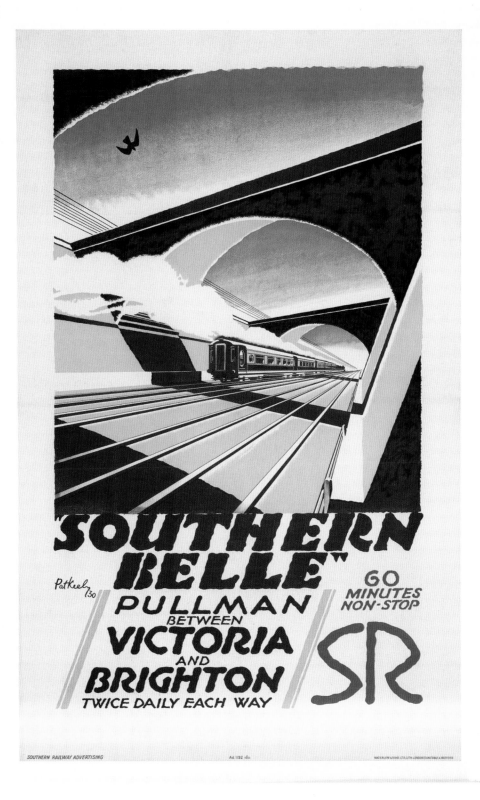

By the late 1920s poster graphics had changed considerably. This abstract, geometric representation of the route to Brighton is a forerunner of the art-deco style that would strongly influence the interior design of the 1933 electric Pullman cars.

Chapter 4
The Sparks Effect

Twenty-six years earlier, on Sunday 26th July 1903, Driver Thompsett was waiting to depart from Victoria station with the 'Brighton Limited'. He had one of the LBSCR's latest express steam locomotives, B4 4-4-0 No. 70 *Holyrood*, at the head of just three Pullmans and a Pup and he had been given instructions from on high to make the run in the shortest possible time. Less than 49 minutes later the train was standing at the platform at Brighton, having reached a top speed of 90 miles per hour on the racing straight through Horley.

This frolic had a serious purpose. The LBSCR Board had been galvanised by a proposal to build a new rival non-stop electric line between London and Brighton and were investigating the potential for electric traction on their own main line and the possibility of a 50-minute timing over the 50 miles to Brighton. It had all started with Magnus Volk, a Victorian inventor with a particular interest in electricity. In 1883 he had opened on Brighton seafront one of the world's first electric railways as a curiosity for visitors – it is still operating today. This practical demonstration had helped to spread the idea of electric traction for railways. London's first electric deep level tube line, the City and South London, opened in 1890. Two years later, Leeds became the first city to operate electric trams and a year after that the all-electric Liverpool Overhead Railway opened.

Volk's Electric Railway. Presented to the people of Brighton by Magnus Volk, an inventor and engineer, on 4th August 1883, this narrow gauge railway is now the world's oldest operating public electric railway. It operates along the Brighton seafront from the Aquarium to Black Rock between Easter and September and is well worth a visit. The photo shows one of the electric cars on the viaduct at Banjo Groyne in Edwardian days. *Volk's Electric Railway Association*

The LBSCR obtained general powers to electrify its network and commissioned the eminent consulting electrical engineer Philip Dawson to advise the Board. The company's Chief Engineer, Charles Morgan, visited Italy to see the newly-electrified line from Milan to Varese, which used the third-rail system, and the Valtellina main line, electrified on the 3600V a.c. three-phase overhead system. He came down firmly in favour of overhead electrification. Advised by Dawson, the LBSCR contracted with the German firm *Allgemeine Electricitäts Gesellschaft* (AEG) to electrify a section of the South London line between Battersea Park and South Bermondsey on the overhead system with a 6,600V a.c. 25Hz single phase supply, but during construction is was decided to electrify the entire route from Victoria to London Bridge.

In the meantime the London County Council's tramway network in south London, electrified from 1903, was offering a clean, modern, convenient and cheap alternative to the steam suburban railways of south London and particularly to the LBSCR's mean and dingy 4-wheel carriages. The competition hit traffic hard, contibuting to a halving of ticket revenue at some inner suburban stations.

Public operation of the new electric services began on 1st December 1909 and traffic began to recover at once, rising by 50% within the first month and doubling by April 1910. The 'sparks effect', stimulating customer demand by offering fast, frequent, clean and bright electric trains, was working. In the next two years the LBSCR extended its electric network from both Victoria and London Bridge to Crystal Palace and Norwood Junction. The company's subsequent project, a further extension of electrification over most of the LBSCR's suburban lines and including SECR services to Caterham and Tattenham Corner, was halted by World War I, which also, unsurprisingly, terminated the relationship with AEG.

Work resumed on the electrification of routes to Coulsdon North and Sutton in 1922 and was completed by the Southern Railway in 1925. Whereas the earlier schemes had used conventional multiple unit arrangements of power cars and trailers, the Coulsdon and Sutton routes were operated with locomotive vans marshalled between trailers, possibly with a view to the eventual use of electric locomotives to Brighton. Another Southern constituent, the London and South Western Railway (LSWR), had also been busy electrifying its principal suburban routes. The LSWR used direct current at a nominal 600 volts, supplied *via* an outside top-contact conductor rail and returned *via* the running rails. It, too, experienced a gratifying surge in traffic as a result.

With these results, the Southern Railway's Board needed no further convincing of the sparks effect. Cleaner, faster, more frequent services attracted traffic that was otherwise being lost to buses and trams. What is more, operating and maintenance costs were far lower, whilst multiple units simplified terminal operations and made more efficient use of track capacity.

But which system to adopt? The company had inherited two different ones and there was a third on the drawing board – 3,000V d.c. four-rail – for the South Eastern and Chatham lines. Of the three, the LSWR's third rail system required the least capital investment per track mile, was the least disruptive to install and represented the largest part of the suburban network already electrified. Accordingly the Southern's Board decided in 1924 that the ex-SECR suburban routes would be electrified on the d.c. third-rail system at 660 volts and that the ex-LBSCR a.c. overhead routes would be converted to the new standard. By 1929 all of the a.c. equipment had been replaced and one year later the project to electrify virtually all of the Southern's inner-suburban network was complete.

Sir Herbert Walker imposed strict financial targets on each electrification scheme. Projects were carried out as economically as possible. Most of the rolling stock was converted from former steam-hauled or a.c. electric cars and existing semaphore signalling was retained wherever traffic densities did not justify an upgrade. On many stations even the original gas lamps remained in use.

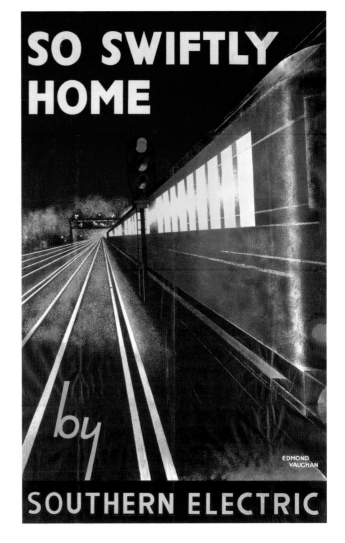

SO SWIFTLY HOME

by

SOUTHERN ELECTRIC

EDMOND VAUGHAN

The Southern strongly promoted its fast, frequent electric train services with posters and booklets extolling the virtues of suburban life, with gratifying financial results for the company. Poster artwork by Edmond Vaughan. *National Railway Museum/Science & Society Picture Library*

Pioneers of electrification. An original LSWR 3-car unit heads a suburban electric train at Hounslow, probably in the late 1920s. *Laurie Mack Collection*

15

Chapter 5
'Gentlemen...'

'Gentlemen, I have decided to electrify to Brighton.' With this startling announcement to the Southern Railway's 1929 Traffic Officers' Conference, Sir Herbert Walker launched Britain's first main line electrification project.

That year the Chancellor, Winston Churchill, had abolished a longstanding tax on First Class fares on condition that the railways used the additional income to fund projects that would help to relieve unemployment. For the Southern, the capitalised future value of the saving was just over £2m. However, the Brighton electrification project would cost about £2.7m – about £135m at today's values[2]. To bridge the gap the new electric services would need to generate 6% more revenue in addition to the expected operating cost savings – in fact they were to generate 19% more revenue from increased traffic by the end of the first year[3].

The Southern's project did more than just electrify the Brighton main line: it transformed the scale and quality of the train service. 'Passengers do not like timetables' was one of Walker's aphorisms so the new electric operation, introduced on 1st January 1933, was based on high-frequency services at easy-to-remember regular intervals. The expresses from Victoria to Brighton were the most memorable of all: 'every hour, on the hour, in the hour'.

Including the direct route from Coulsdon North, the limit of the existing suburban electric network, to Brighton, the Quarry line bypass to the Redhill bottleneck, the lines from Redhill to Reigate and from Preston Park to West Worthing, the Southern electrified over 160 track miles under this scheme. The Central Electricity Board grid delivered power at 33kV a.c. to the railway at three points from which it was cabled to 18 unmanned rectifier substations that supplied 660V d.c. to the third rail, the whole operation being supervised from an electrical control room at Three Bridges.

South of Coulsdon, traffic had been controlled by semaphore signalling using the 'absolute block' principle, whereby only one train could occupy a line between two adjacent manned signal-boxes. As these could be two or more miles apart, the system limited the capacity of the route. The Southern

replaced most of the semaphore signalling between Coulsdon and Brighton with semi-automatic three-aspect colour light signals operated by track circuits. With the exceptions of the long Quarry and Clayton tunnels, each of which was a single block section, the new colour light signals were spaced at intervals of between 1,400 and 1,500 yards to accommodate the new, more intensive train service. The company rebuilt Haywards Heath station with two island platforms, remodelled Brighton station to provide longer platforms and to simplify the track layout.

The Southern decided to use multiple units for the new service, for expresses as well as for local services. There were several reasons for this. First, multiple units eliminate the need to attach and detach locomotives at each end of the journey, freeing track capacity at Victoria, Brighton and London Bridge. The process of lengthening and shortening trains for peak and off-peak traffic levels is similarly simplified and portions of trains can be split and joined to serve two destinations. Second, all of the available platform space at terminals can be used for passenger-carrying vehicles – the 'dead' space for a locomotive at each end is eliminated. Third, multiple unit trains have broadly constant power-to-weight ratios regardless of length so timetabling and performance are standardised. Finally, multiple units have power collection 'shoes' along the length of the train making it easier to cope with the inevitable gaps in the electrified third rail at junctions – potentially a critical factor when accelerating a heavy train through the complex points and crossings outside Victoria station on the steep climb to Grosvenor bridge.

Whereas most of the Southern's suburban electric multiple units were low-cost rebuilds of old locomotive-hauled coaches, the Brighton line fleets were to be all-new. To this end, during 1932 passengers on the Cobham line caught occasional glimpses of a strange-looking electric train undergoing trials. Unlike the bull-nosed suburban units that were then the mainstay of this route, the powered cars at each end had a well-proportioned but much flatter front with a domed roof. These cars were brand new and resembled the Southern's latest Third Class saloons for main line steam trains. Instead of the usual truss-frame between the bogies these cars had a mysterious collection of equipment boxes instead – Cobham line passengers were used to such things being tidied away at the

---

2 Based on share of GDP – calculated using www.measuringworth.com
3 Dendy Marshall, C. revised by Kidner, R.: 'A History of the Southern Railway'. Ian Allan 1968 p412

On the last lap. Unit No. 2053 is depicted south of Clayton tunnel, between Hassocks and Preston Park, and heads down the gentle 1 in 264 gradient towards Brighton. Note the lofty telegraph poles, and power cables which are carried in trunking beside the line. This photograph is believed to have been taken in 1934. *Lens of Sutton*

back of driving compartments. Between them were marshalled two specially constructed coaches with LSWR bodies, lengthened by new sections to Maunsell profile and mounted on new underframes, and between these an unidentified Maunsell corridor Third. Control cabling snaked down the corridors to link the driving motored cars at each end.

Satisfied with the outcome of these trials, the Southern placed orders for its new express electric fleets. The mainstay of the route was to be twenty 6-car units, each consisting of two driving motor brake saloon Thirds flanking four unpowered ('trailer') cars, a compartment Third, two compartment composites and a Pullman car. As with the existing steam-hauled service, the Pullman Car Company would continue to

provide on-board catering on all of the new electric expresses. Three more 6-car units, principally for the 'City Limited' commuter service from Brighton to London Bridge, were generally similar but the three non-Pullman trailers were all First Class.

As well as these 6-car express units, the Southern built a new fleet of 4-car units for semi-fast and stopping services. These were a superior form of the company's suburban stock, having non-corridor compartments in three cars and a side corridor linking the compartments to two lavatories in the fourth car, though one had to be something of a trainspotter to know which car to travel in if one anticipated the need for relief en route!

Chapter 6
The Electric Belle

The steam-hauled all-Pullman Southern Belle had been a commercial success and had conferred prestige on both organisations so, naturally, both the Southern Railway and the Pullman Car Company wanted the service to continue after electrification of the Brighton Line. The question was, how best to achieve this? Continuing with steam haulage of the existing Pullman cars was both operationally unsatisfactory and risked the Southern Belle appearing old-fashioned alongside the Southern's brand-new 6-car express electric multiple units. And, if new Pullmans were to be built for an electrically-powered Belle, the arguments for multiple unit, rather than electric locomotive, operation were the same as for the Southern's other Brighton expresses.

The two companies agreed to build three all-Pullman electric multiple units – the first such trains in the world – to operate the Southern Belle. The units were similar to the new Brighton line express fleet and had the same running gear, electrical and pneumatic systems, financed and maintained by the Southern Railway. The Southern also provided motormen (the term used to describe electric train drivers) and guards, whilst the Pullman Car Company funded and maintained the car bodies and provided the on-board service to passengers.

The three Belle units each consisted of five cars, all of which were built during 1932 by Metropolitan-Cammell at their Saltley works. Like the motor coaches and the individual Pullmans in the twenty-three 6-car express units, the Belle cars were constructed entirely of steel, something of an innovation as most passenger coaches of the period had a wooden body frame with steel panelling. Each unit was 346ft long, 9ft wide, 12ft 5in high and weighed 250 tons.

The two driving motor brake cars both had two 9ft two-axle bogies, each axle having a 225 horsepower (hp) British Thomson-Houston (BTH) type 163 traction motor, suspended from the bogie frame and mounted on the axle by means of a bearing. The motor drove the axle through reduction gears that gave a top speed of about 75mph on level track. Thus, the four powered bogies on the two driving motor brake cars developed a total of 1,800 installed hp.

Each of the motor coach bogies had shoe-beams mounted on both sides to collect electricity from the 660 volt third-rail

supply and feed it to a power bus-line running the length of the unit, with jumper cables connecting each car to the next. As well as feeding the traction control equipment on each motor coach, the power bus-line fed a motor-generator set on each of the driving motor brake cars. This delivered a 70 volt supply for control systems, brake compressors, train lighting and other auxiliary systems. The power bus-line also supplied a dynamotor under the floor of each First Class trailer car that provided a 110 volt supply for the all-electric kitchen.

Inside each cab was a 'master controller' that enabled the motorman to control the supply of power to the motors in order to regulate the train's speed. The motorman activated ('cut in') the controller in the leading cab by inserting a key. As the motorman moved the handle of the master controller through a quadrant he energised a series of circuits in a multi-core control cable that ran the length of the train and operated the traction control equipment on each power car. The master controller was also known as the 'dead man's handle' because the motorman had to hold it down under spring pressure when driving. If an incapacitated driver released it, the traction current to the motors would be cut and an automatic emergency brake application would be made. The traction control equipment, supplied by Metropolitan-Vickers, consisted of electro-pneumatic contactors that arranged the two motors on each bogie electrically either in series or in parallel and that switched line power through a grid of resistances.

Initially the motors would be connected in series, thereby halving the supply voltage to each motor, and all of the resistances would be connected in series, so reducing the voltage across the motors to a fraction of the line voltage. This was necessary because applying full voltage to a motor that has to overcome the inertia of a stationary train before it can turn would cause a flashover that would severely damage the motor. As the train accelerated the resistances would be progressively switched out until the full line power was being supplied to each pair of in-series motors. These would then be switched to parallel, with all of the resistances back in circuit and the switching-out process would again be carried out until each motor was at full line power. There was a separate reverser control circuit to change the direction of operation of the motors on each power car. Although the Southern's contemporary suburban fleets had contactors that were opened by springs and closed by electro-magnets, on the new Brighton express stock the contactors were, for the first time, operated by compressed air working in cylinders and operating on pistons. Electro-magnets, activated by the 70 volt control circuits, operated the cylinder air valves.

Because the control equipment on the three Belle units was identical to that on the Southern's six-car Brighton express units, the two fleets could work in multiple with each other and with later builds of pre-war Southern express units. To enable coupled units to be linked electrically, each unit had a single multi-core control jumper cable mounted on the offside and a corresponding receptacle on the nearside. There were no inter-unit power cables but the units did have a receptacle to enable a cable from an overhead power trolley to be connected in order to move them in and out of depots where a third rail would be hazardous.

A characteristic sound of the Southern Electric system was the ringing thump of an electrically operated reciprocating compressor under each motor coach as it periodically topped up the main air reservoir for the Westinghouse automatic air brake. These reservoirs were linked along the train and also supplied the air for the whistle and the electro-pneumatic contactors that operated the traction control equipment.

When the motorman moved his brake valve to the 'release and running' position, it charged a second 'brake' pipe with compressed air and this in turn filled auxiliary reservoirs on each coach through a device called a triple valve, which also vented the brake cylinder to atmosphere. When the motorman moved his brake valve to the 'service application' position it allowed air from the brake pipe to escape to the atmosphere in a controlled manner. The triple valve in each coach sensed this reduction in pressure, closed the feeds from the brake pipe to the auxiliary cylinder and from the brake cylinder to atmosphere and opened a feed from the auxiliary cylinder to the brake cylinder, forcing the piston outwards to operate a mechanical linkage that applied brake blocks to the rim of each wheel. The pressure differential between the brake pipe and the auxiliary cylinders controlled the strength of the brake application; when the two pressures were again balanced the triple valves would stop feeding air to the brake cylinders.

If the motorman placed his brake valve handle in the 'emergency application' position, all of the air in the brake pipe would be released, slamming on the brakes on all cars. The same would happen if the motorman released the dead-man's handle or if a brake-pipe burst, for example because a coupling broke. The guard could also apply the brake via an emergency cock, and the passengers and Pullman attendants by pulling the communication cord. The motorman would place his

Cab of 11201, part of the Southern Electric Group's preserved pre-war Southern Railway express unit 3142. The electrical control equipment was supplied in 1938 by English Electric but is generally similar to the controls of the Belle units. The master controller, also known as the 'dead man's handle' was spring-loaded and had to be held down quite firmly to prevent the emergency brake applying – motormen needed strong arms! The Forward/Reverse switch is to the left of the master controller lever and the brake valve is to the far left. On the wall to the left of the controls, above the driver's position, were three gauges, an ammeter (top), a speedometer (centre) and a duplex brake pressure gauge (bottom). To the right of the driving position was a handbrake consisting of a pedestal with a vertically mounted rotating handle. *Simon Jeffs*

Photo of driving Motor Brake car, highlighting shoegear, and control cables.

brake valve handle to the 'lap' position to prevent the possibility of recharging the train brake pipe, and releasing the brake. When the motorman again placed his brake valve handle in the 'release and running' position, compressed air from the main brake reservoirs was again allowed to enter the brake pipe. As the pressure in this pipe rose along the train, the triple valve on each coach would exhaust the compressed air in the brake cylinder, producing a series of hissing sighs from the front to the rear of the train, and re-charge the auxiliary cylinder on each coach ready for the next brake application.

Chapter 7
Designed for Comfort

Each 5-car Belle unit was made up of two Driving Motor Brake Parlour Third Class cars, a Trailer Parlour Third and two Trailer Kitchen Firsts, with a total capacity of 40 First Class and 152 Third Class seats. Bodywork was based on contemporary Pullman car design, having a large, rectangular window to each seating bay that incorporated horizontally sliding glazed ventilators and recessed, inwards-opening external passenger doors with deep, oval windows. The units were painted in Pullman umber livery, lined in gold, with cream panels between the windows. The Pullman coat of arms was displayed centrally on the front of each driving motor brake car and at both ends of the bodyside of each car.

Pullman practice was to bestow individual names on cars that included First Class accommodation and to prominently display them centrally on the lower bodysides. In keeping with the Belle theme, these and the composite Pullman cars formed in the other Brighton express units were given popular girls' names of the era rather than the traditional Pullman mix of royalty, deities and exotic places. The Third Class cars carried a similarly prominent bodyside legend based on the last two digits of the car's number in the Pullman Car Company's asset schedule, for example 'CAR NO 85 THIRD CLASS', later shortened to 'CAR NO 85'. Each car's full schedule number was displayed on a small cast data plate above the buffers at each end (photo below right).

Each car had pressure ventilation, with fresh air drawn in from outside and passed through a chamber where it was heated electrically in cold weather. To reduce interior noise levels, the floors had cork insulation whilst the majority of the sides and most of the roof area were insulated by thick layers of 'Insulwood', with an air space between each layer.

The Driving Motor Brake Parlour Thirds at each end of each unit consisted of a full width driving cab with inwards opening doors. The cab, which was identical to those in the Southern's other Brighton express units, had a tip-up seat (many motormen preferred to drive standing) and a pedestal with the master controller and brake valve. These, together with an ammeter, a duplex gauge showing pressures in the main air pipe and the brake pipe and a speedometer (reputedly never actually connected), were on the left side of the cab as most signals and platforms were on this side.

A separate pedestal was provided on the other side of the cab for the handbrake; the window on this side was hinged on one side to enable the motorman to change the stencil headcode clipped to the outside of the light-box mounted centrally between the cab windows. The Southern had a system of single-character headcodes for its suburban network but adopted double-digit numbers for the Brighton line and subsequent main line electrifications. '4' (with a blank for the second number space) was the designation for Victoria-Brighton or

1932 unit No.	2051	2052	2053	Seats	
1937 unit No.	3051	3052	3053	1st	3rd
Driving Motor Brake Parlour Third	Car No. (2)88	Car No. (2)90	Car No. (2)92		48
Trailer Kitchen First	(279) 'Hazel'	(284) 'Vera'	(281) 'Gwen'	20	
Trailer Kitchen First	(282) 'Doris'	(280) 'Audrey'	(283) 'Mona'	20	
Trailer Parlour Third	Car No. (2)86	Car No. (2)87	Car No. (2)85		56
Driving Motor Brake Parlour Third	Car No. (2)89	Car No. (2)91	Car No. (2)93		48
			TOTAL	40	152

The distinctive external passenger door with its characteristic oval window is seen on Trailer Kitchen First car 'Doris' (formerly in unit 3051) at Horsted Keynes on the Bluebell Railway on 26th June 2009. The car's end gangway has been removed. *Colin Duff*

Left: Second Class car as refurbished in 1968. *Doug Lindsay Collection*

Brighton-Victoria non-stop services via the Quarry Line and was therefore the usual headcode for the Brighton Belle. The purpose of these headcodes, which were removed at the end of each journey, was to indicate the train's route and stopping pattern to signalmen, although many regular passengers used them to identify 'their' train.

There was an internal door on the offside of the cab, leading into a guard's/luggage compartment which had double external doors, both of which opened outwards. A seat and a desk were provided for the guard and a periscope arrangement to roof level so that the guard could view signals – part of the guard's duties in those days was to monitor progress and double-check signals, especially on the approach to junctions. The guard also had a duplex brake pressure gauge and a brake valve for use in an emergency.

As there was no vestibule at the outer end of the passenger

saloon, the partition between the guard's compartment and the passenger accommodation incorporated a central emergency exit door. Two 3-bay Third Class saloons ('parlours' in Pullman terminology) had a total of 48 seats arranged 2+2 either side of a central gangway in facing pairs with tables. At the inner end of the car was a passageway with lavatory compartment on one side and two small storage cupboards and a ventilation equipment cupboard on the other. The passageway led into a transverse entrance vestibule with inward opening doors with oval glazing, oval end windows and a corridor connection to the next car. The tare weight of each of these cars was 62 tons and each was 66ft 9ins long.

The cupboard, lavatory and vestibule arrangement was similar at each end of the Trailer Parlour Third, which seated 56 in a four-bay and a three-bay saloon with a central partition. This car weighed 39 tons tare and was 66ft long.

Each unit included two First Class Kitchen Trailers with end vestibules and corridor connections. These flanked a small all-electric kitchen, a pantry and two 2-bay saloons each with eight seats arranged 1+1 either side of a central gangway, a 4-seat coupé and a lavatory. The tare weight of each of these cars was 43 tons, they were 66ft long and were marshalled in a pair with the kitchens at the outer ends.

Interiors were sumptuous and ornate, with subtle Art Deco touches. It is a tradition of Pullman craftsmanship to give each car its own individual decorative character and each of the 15 Belle cars was unique, if only in some small variation in its elaborate hand-crafted marquetry panelling. For example a contemporary account described the interior of 'Doris' as:

'... treated with fine English walnut of three varieties of figures, and the panels are quartered and cross-banded. The decorative effect is obtained by the use of Convex Eagle mirrors, cut in fine boxwood with black beaded rims, and also by the introduction of etchings mounted in black mouldings. The carpets are of rich deep pile in tones of green. The chair and seat coverings are in moquette velvet, in tones of brown, red and fawn', and 'Gwen' as:

'... the main panel work is in figured English walnut with lace wood and laurel lines. Marquetry work is introduced in the principal panels, and carried out in boxwood, weathered sycamore and red and white natural pear-wood ... the carpet is of Wilton pile, in tones of blue, whilst the chairs are covered in velvet moquette in blue and mauve tints.'[4]

Metalwork was finished in satin silver and each glass-topped table was provided with a classic Pullman table lamp with a tulip-shaped celluloid shade. An electric bell system was linked to a coloured light panel that indicated the location of the call to the attendant. In First Class cars, ceiling lights were enclosed in peach-coloured frosted glass strips whilst in Third Class the effect of the semi-recessed ceiling bulbs was softened by down-lighters on side and end panels.

4 *The Locomotive*, 14 January 1933, quoted in Charles Fryer; 'British Pullman Trains', Silver Link Publishing, 1992.

First Class car 'Gwen'. The absence of window curtains indicates this is a pre-war picture. *Doug Lindsay Collection*

Opposite: First Class car 'Vera' in original condition. *Doug Lindsay Collection*

First Class car 'Audrey' in original condition. *Doug Lindsay Collection*   Opposite: First Class car 'Doris'. *Doug Lindsay Collection*

Third Class car No. 87 when new. *Doug Lindsay Collection*

Opposite: One of the two saloons of First Class car 'Doris'. *Colin Duff*

Centre opposite: The glass diffusers over the parlour car ceiling lights were decorated with an art-deco sunburst pattern. *Simon Jeffs, artefact from the collection of Antony Ford*

Above: The sunburst pattern was repeated on the downlighters from Third Class cars. *Simon Jeffs, artefact from the collection of Antony Ford*

Right: ... and even the door handles. *Simon Jeffs, artefact from the collection of Antony Ford*

Upper far right: The iconic Pullman lamp with tulip-shaped shade. *Simon Jeffs, artefact from the collection of Antony Ford*

Far right: Each lamp was allocated to an individual car, and was identified with a stamp on the base. The example shown is from 'Audrey'. *Simon Jeffs, artefact from the collection of Antony Ford*

Opposite: The lighting diffusers in 'Doris' and clock above the doorway. *Colin Duff*

Right: Each seat was numbered. *Colin Duff*

Far right: The bell to summon the attendant was set in the car wall. *Colin Duff*

Chapter 8
The Belle Enters Service

Electrification, with its frequent services and high quality rolling stock, provided a much-needed economic boost to Brighton and its neighbours. The Mayor of Brighton, Councillor Frank G. Beal, J.P., congratulated the Southern Railway 'on their vision and enterprise and the South Coast resorts upon the new asset of incalculable value which the Company had presented to them as a New Year's gift'.

The new Brighton line timetable, launched on Sunday 1st January 1933, had an express service each hour throughout the day. Of these, the 11.00am, 3.00pm and 7.00pm departures from Victoria and the 1.25pm, 5.25pm and 9.25pm return departures were Southern Belle all-Pullman services. All were non-stop and shown in the public timetable as completing the journey in exactly 60 minutes – the working timetable generally had the services arriving a minute or two earlier. Two of the three units were kept overnight under cover in the station platforms at Victoria and taken out to the Battersea Pier carriage sidings every weekday morning to get them out of the way of the peak commuter traffic, after which they returned to the station in good time for the 11.00am Brighton service.

New and old at Victoria. On 1st January 1933 the new Southern Belle stands in Platform 17 at Victoria Station whilst a 30-year old ex-LSWR Drummond S11 heads a train over the yet to be electrified Mid-Sussex route.

Once the 11.00am service had arrived at Brighton, the pair of units ran empty to the Southern's electric multiple unit depot at Lovers' Walk, where they were split. One unit remained at the depot for maintenance whilst the other returned to the station to work the 1.25pm service to Victoria solo. On returning from Victoria at 4.00pm, it was coupled to the previous day's maintenance unit for the 5.25pm run back up to town. On arrival at Victoria, the two units split again. One unit shunted back to the carriage sidings returning later to the platforms to stable overnight. The other operated the 7.00pm service to Brighton, returning to Victoria at 9.25pm to be re-united with the first unit and stabled overnight in the platform at Victoria. However these arrangements were flexible and adjusted according to anticipated loadings and the spare unit was often kept at Streatham Hill depot in south London.

As with locomotive hauled Pullman cars, the Southern Railway was responsible for operations and for maintaining the underframes, bogies and traction equipment of the 5-car Belle units. The bodies and interior fittings were maintained by Pullman at its works at Preston Park, Brighton, set up in 1928 in part of the former LBSCR's workshops and stores. The two units that were normally in traffic rotated with a third that was held spare or undergoing routine maintenance at Lovers' Walk, which dealt with one unit per day from Monday to Saturday. The Belle units would also occasionally visit the Southern's depot at Peckham Rye for major overhauls to running gear and electrical equipment and for repairs that could not be undertaken at Lovers' Walk.

From 1931, when the all-Pullman Bournemouth Belle had started running, the Southern Belle was no longer the only Belle on the Southern Railway. Accordingly, in a ceremony at Brighton station on 29th June 1934, the then Lady Mayor of Brighton, Miss M. Hardy, renamed the service the Brighton Belle, a title that the train would carry for the rest of its 38-year life.

The scene at Victoria on 29th June 1934 when the Southern Belle was renamed the Brighton Belle. *Getty Images*

Electrification of the Brighton main line had been a huge financial success and, despite the difficult economic times, the Southern's Chairman, Sir Herbert Walker, persuaded the Board to electrify the line from Haywards Heath (Keymer Junction) to Eastbourne and onwards to Hastings and Ore, a project that was completed in July 1935. For this extension the Southern Railway procured seventeen more 6-car electric express units to augment its existing twenty-three-strong fleet.

As before, the on-board catering on the Eastbourne route would be in the hands of the Pullman Car Company. However, financing fifteen new cars for the Brighton Belle and a further twenty-three for the other express units of the 1933 scheme had so over-stretched the Pullman company's finances that it had had to negotiate deferred payments with the car builders. This time the Southern Railway agreed to provide the catering facilities on the new fleet, which simply consisted of a pantry (kitchenette) and counter, staffed by a Pullman steward and providing a limited range of light refreshments.

Until these new units joined the fleet, the three Brighton Belle units had been designated '5 PUL' in operating publications and the 6-car units with a single Pullman car were coded '6 COR' or '6 COR*'. To distinguish the two 6-car fleets the 6 COR units were recoded to '6 PUL' or '6 CIT', the new fleet was described as '6 PAN' and the Brighton Belle all-Pullman units became '5 BEL'. The 6-car fleets were pooled in order to provide Pullman cars on Brighton, Eastbourne and Worthing routes and '6 PUL/6 PAN' became the standard formation for the majority of twelve-car trains.

The Brighton Belle fleet underwent a further change of identity at the beginning of 1937. As the range of unit numbers for suburban electrics (1201-1999) was becoming overcrowded, the number series 2001-2999 was assigned to fleets that were intended primarily for main-line stopping services but were technically compatible with the suburban fleets. To make room, existing gangwayed express units (which could not operate in multiple with suburban-type units) were renumbered in the 3001-3999 series and the three Brighton Belle units accordingly changed from 2051-2053 to 3051-3053.

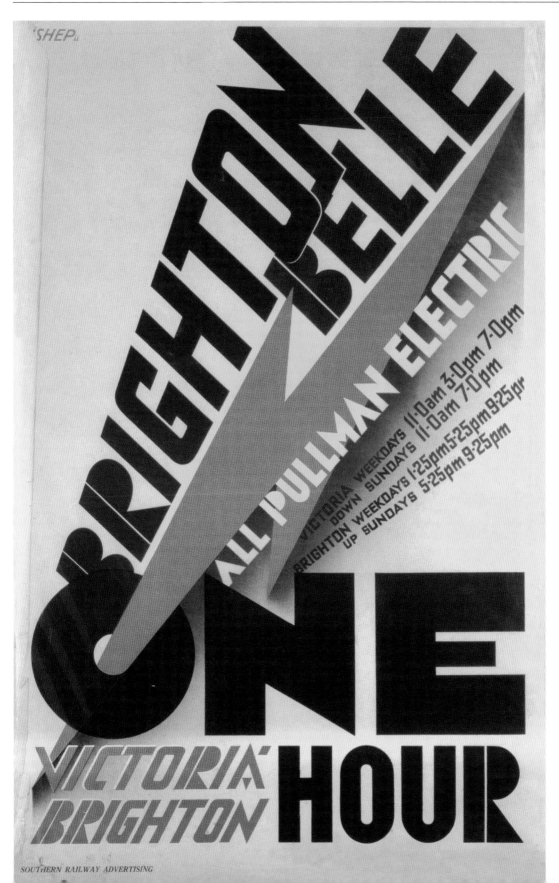

Chapter 9
A Trip to Brighton – 1936

Let us take a trip to Brighton. Shortly before 11am on a weekday morning in the late summer of 1936, we make our way over the crowded concourse of London's Victoria station to platform 17. After showing our Third Class tickets at the barrier, we walk to the front of the 10-car Pullman train where the attendant at the door invites us to sit where we like as it will not be very busy today.

Passing through the vestibule with its oval windows and turning left through the narrow passageway, we enter a saloon with groups of four seats, each with its own table adorned by a silver Art Deco lamp and covered with a crisp, white tablecloth already laid for morning coffee. Squeezing into the seats we look around at the interior. Even in Third Class, each car has its own decorative style, though less elaborate than those of the First Class cars. In this one, the designer has wholeheartedly embraced the latest trends, with wall panelling enlivened by marquetry sunbursts in contrasting Empire hardwoods, satin silver luggage racks, and the seats trimmed in a strident 'jazz' pattern moquette.

As the clock over the doorway at the end of the saloon shows 11am the train moves off. We notice how effective the sound insulation is as she glides slowly over the complex pointwork of the station throat. On the South Eastern lines over to our left, another Pullman train – the 'Golden Arrow' – is departing for Dover, its olive-green 'Lord Nelson' class steam locomotive making heavy weather of the short, sharp climb to Grosvenor bridge over the Thames. No such problems for us, with 3,600 horsepower and 16 driving axles for our 10-car train we soon leave the 'Golden Arrow' struggling in our wake. A brief glimpse of the 'Temple of Power', Sir Giles Gilbert Scott's impressive new Battersea power station with its two smoking chimneys, then a long, right-hand downward swoop past the soot-blackened terraced houses of Battersea before we again turn towards the south beyond Clapham Junction.

As London's slums give way to elegant, spacious Victorian and Edwardian villas we reflect that it was the railway that made it possible for well-to-do families and their servants to move out to the health-giving fresh air of the suburbs whilst father commuted by steam train to his office in the City. Those trains are electric now; faster, cleaner and more frequent, and what had once been open fields beyond London are rapidly being developed with huge new estates of semi-detached houses for clerks, typists and shop-workers. New factories on modern suburban industrial estates are producing consumer goods such as radios, vacuum cleaners and washing machines that will be powered by electricity from the new National Grid. Arterial roads link the new developments and more and more middle-class families are buying their first car. There are no rail links to those new factories and the companies' fleets of road vans transport their goods to the warehouses and shops.

It is an age of transport wonders. Electric trains may no longer be a novelty but an electric Pullman express certainly is. The giant new Cunard liner 'Queen Mary' has just won the Blue Riband with the first westbound crossing of the Atlantic in just under four days. Imperial Airways is operating from Croydon Aerodrome to destinations in Africa and India and has now linked with the newly-formed QANTAS airline to provide a through service from London to Brisbane in just twelve days.

Our musings are abruptly ended by a series of shuddering crashes as the heavy motor bogies of our leading Pullman car negotiate Coulsdon North Junction where the slow Brighton lines diverge from ours to take the 'old' route via Redhill. The attendant, who knew what was coming, had braced himself against our table as he deftly poured our fresh coffee but, as we plunge into the darkness of the Cane Hill covered way in the grounds of the large asylum on the slopes of the Coulsdon hills, wavelets of coffee transfer themselves from cups to saucers and so back to the Pullman Company via the tablecloth.

Now we are on the so-called Quarry line, which is part of the continuous four-track railway completed in 1911 from Victoria to Balcombe Tunnel Junction. Plans were drawn up to extend quadrupling on to Brighton, but the costs of extra tunnels through the South Downs were deemed too great, and the line south of Three Bridges remains a bottleneck. The Quarry line crosses over the slow lines at Star Lane, then takes a more easterly course. A deep chalk cutting heralds our approach to Quarry tunnel and we emerge to glimpse Merstham station to our right which only serves the slow lines. Whilst building the Quarry line, the LBSCR received a request from the eccentric owner of Hooley Court, who wished the railway to paint all the telegraph poles within sight of his house green and to affix Union Jack flags atop each!

His request was officially 'mislaid'. The Holmethorpe Works of British Industrial Sand gives its name to the short Redhill Sand tunnel, where the former South Eastern Railway line to Tonbridge and on to Dover passes over us. This was part of the first route from London to Dover, bypassed in 1868 when the Sevenoaks cut-off was opened.

Our route again runs parallel with the slow lines for the almost straight, gently descending racing stretch from Earlswood to Three Bridges. We are on time so our driver holds the speed below the official maximum of 75mph but even so the ride is lively. Salfords station on our right was originally a private halt for workers at the adjacent Monotype printing equipment factory but was opened to the public with the extension of electrification to Three Bridges in 1932. The large station at Horley, similar in style to those between East Croydon and Balham and dating from the quadrupling of 1905, passes in a flash, followed in quick succession by Gatwick Racecourse station and the newly-opened Gatwick Airport station, linked by a subway direct into the brand-new, avant-garde 'Beehive' air terminal with a solitary de Havilland DH84 biplane outside. Will Gatwick ever replace Croydon as London's main airport, we wonder?

Another series of lurches and thumps from the equalising beams of the bogies and we are through Three Bridges.

Turning our attention from the scene outside to our morning papers and the world seems an increasingly threatening place. Under Mussolini's dictatorship, Italy has completed its annexation of Abyssinia, showing the League of Nations to be impotent. In Spain, General Franco is mounting a military *coup d'etat* against the newly-elected left-wing government and civil war seems likely. Neville Chamberlain is urging 'restraint' as Hitler's Germany consolidates its reoccupation of the Rhineland by building extensive fortifications. What is not in the newspapers, though it is widely publicised in America with much speculation about the relationship, is any mention of King Edward VIII's Mediterranean yachting cruise in the company of Mrs Wallis Simpson. Monarchs, it seems, no longer conduct their amorous affairs in Brighton.

We note that the countryside passing our window is changing in character, the chalk of the North Downs and flat farmland of the Weald giving way to the sandstone ridge of the Ardingly beds and the High Weald of Sussex. The trees of Tilgate and Worth forests close in on both sides, four lines become two and we plunge into the long and damp Balcombe tunnel. Over our heads, the nascent tributaries of the River Mole drip through the porous sandstone, causing so much trouble to the electrics in the tunnel that it is lined with metal sheeting.

Photographic perfection. The graceful curve of the arches framing the train, deep cutting, wooded background and lack of foreground intrusion; one can see why this location, just south of The Quarry tunnel, was a favourite with official photographers for publicity shots. The train appears to be the 3.00pm Victoria to Brighton and this gem of a photograph was taken in 1937. *Lens of Sutton Association*

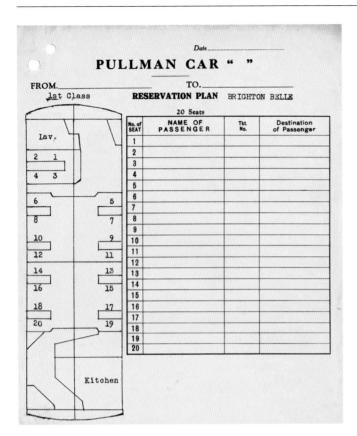

More paperwork! First and Third Class seat reservation cards for the Belle's attendants. *Simon Jeffs (photo) from the Antony Ford Collection*

Shaking off a few droplets of water, the Belle is now deep in glorious Sussex countryside. The quaint, country station of Balcombe comes and goes and then we are on the major engineering feature of the line, the Ouse Viaduct. Described as 'one of the most magnificent undertakings ever constructed' at the time of its completion, it is 462 yards long, up to 100 feet high and supported on 37 arches. The balustrades are of Caen stone and there are four small classical pavilions at each end, eight in all. Below can be seen the infant waters of the River Ouse that will eventually reach the sea at Newhaven. To the left are the red brick buildings of Ardingly College and to the right, over a sea of oak trees, is the Nymans Estate. Our coffee cups pause in mid-air as we drink in this scene of perfect rural Englishness.

Up and Down loops appear, to serve two of the four platforms of the busy commuter railhead of Haywards Heath, then after a short tunnel, we are on the last leg of our journey to Brighton. Our plates are collected as we pass through the quaint station named Wivelsfield (actually in the Burgess Hill suburb of World's End, but this wasn't thought to be a particularly suitable name for a station!) and Keymer Junction where the line to Newhaven, Eastbourne and Ore diverges, then Burgess Hill and Hassocks.

Ahead is the looming mass of the South Downs and what appears to be the entrance to a castle. This is quickly revealed as the northern portal of Clayton tunnel, the longest on the line at 2,259 yards and built in a flamboyant crenellated style complete with cottage between the two turrets. Clayton Tunnel's other claim to fame is more sombre as it was the scene of a dreadful accident on Sunday 25th August 1861 when two trains collided inside the tunnel with the loss of 23 lives. The fault lay with the primitive signalling then in force and led to improvements in procedures and technology that continue to this day, making rail travel a very safe mode of transport. The line descends through a deep cutting, then, after one more short tunnel at Patcham, we enter the suburbs of Brighton.

Our attendant discreetly brings our attention to payment of our bill as the Belle slows through Preston Park station where the line to Worthing and Littlehampton diverges to our right. Brighton is a major railway centre and we pass on our right the Pullman Company works and the servicing depot at Lovers' Walk, while to our left is the Brighton works.

As the train glides to a halt under the echoing roof of Brighton station we ease ourselves out of our seats, recover our possessions, bid farewell to our attendant and step down on to the platform. Since electrification Brighton has become one of the busiest stations in the British Isles, with frequent services to London and points west and east along the Sussex coast, plus country routes to Horsham via Shoreham and Steyning, and Tunbridge Wells via Lewes and Uckfield as well as the short, steep branch line to Devil's Dyke. Brighton's other suburban route to Kemp Town closed to passenger traffic when the new main line electric service was inaugurated in January 1933.

However, our journey is over and as we emerge on to Queen's Road, we can see right down the hill to the sea, sparkling in the sun. For all the criticism it received at the time, there is no doubt that Rennie picked an excellent spot for his station although the long, mainly uphill toil for the return journey as the minutes ticked away before one's train departed has doubtless tried generations of weary families!

Vintage 'Belle'. The 5.25pm Brighton to Victoria makes a fine sight as it leaves Patcham tunnel, on the outskirts of Brighton, on 30th June 1935. Note that many passengers appear to have pulled the window blinds down to shield their eyes from the sun. *Locomotive Club of Great Britain Ken Nunn collection*

Chapter 10
War and Peace

On declaration of war with Germany in September 1939, the Government placed the railways under the control of the Ministry of Transport, with a Railway Executive Committee (which had been set up in September 1938) to manage them in support of the war effort. Initially the train service was drastically reduced and all Pullman and other catering services were withdrawn but, as the 'phoney war' progressed, this appeared to be an over-reaction and some Pullman services, including Brighton Belle workings, were reinstated on 1st January 1940. Usually a single 5 BEL unit worked in tandem with a 6 PUL or 6 PAN unit to provide both Pullman and non-Pullman accommodation.

However, in September 1940 the 'blitz' on London that was to last until May 1941 began in earnest. At 10.25pm on 9th October 1940, high-explosive bombs fell through the roof of Victoria station where Brighton Belle stock was berthed as usual at Platform 17. Here, 5 BEL unit 3052 was badly knocked about, car 90 being reported as the most seriously damaged. 3052 was removed to the large and under-utilised Crystal Palace (High Level) station where it was stored under tarpaulins for the duration.

Pullman and other catering services were again withdrawn from May 1942 and units 3051 and 3053 were then also stored. Pullman and other catering services were restored in May 1946 but it was not until 7th October of that year that a Belle unit, 3051, re-entered traffic. 3051 ran for a short time as a six-car unit with trailers 'Doris', 'Hazel', 'Mona' and 'Gwen' until 3053 re-joined the fleet the following month.

The Southern Railway suffered dreadful losses of rolling stock during the Second World War and the Brighton Belle units were not entirely immune, though no vehicle was completely lost. Unit No. 3052 was the worst affected, Pullman car 'Audrey', part of which is visible on the right, being badly damaged in an air raid on Victoria station on 9th October 1940, while car No. 90 (which is thought to be the adjacent vehicle) suffered severe structural damage. This picture provides an excellent view of an equalising-beam 'Dutch' bogie, the riding qualities of which were the source of numerous complaints. *Bluebell Railway Museum*

On 20th July 1951 HRH Princess Elizabeth travelled from Waterloo to Portsmouth and back for a series of engagements and rode in unit No. 3052 which is seen here passing Vauxhall on a rather dull morning. The unit had been beautifully prepared for this duty; the bodywork seems to have been polished to perfection. Appearances of 5 BEL units on the South Western Lines were extremely rare and confined to special workings such as that seen in this picture. Further information on these special duties will be found in chapter 13.
Dennis Cullum/ Lens of Sutton Association

In 1948 a new, regular diagram for a 'Belle' unit was introduced from Victoria to Eastbourne. This working was confined to summer Sundays only, leaving London at 10.40am and running non-stop to Eastbourne in 80 min; the return working left the Sussex coast at 5.45pm, arriving in Victoria at 7.05pm. Declining patronage eventually led to the train being withdrawn at the end of the 1957 season. In this illustration unit No. 3053 is seen galloping along in the evening sunshine, forming the 5.45pm *ex*-Eastbourne, near Berwick on 27th August 1950. *J.J.Smith collection/Bluebell Railway Museum*

Most of the Brighton Line was re-signalled with colour lights in the 1930s, but certain sections in the London suburban area were omitted and, due to the intervention of the Second World War, remained semaphore signalled well into the 1950s. The stretches from Bricklayers Arms Junction to Norwood Junction and Battersea Park to Coulsdon North were dealt with in stages, the final phase being replacement of semaphore signals from Windmill Bridge Junction (near East Croydon) to Coulsdon North which linked up with the existing colour-light signalling to Brighton. This last stage was completed in May 1955. Here (what appears to be) the evening up train from Brighton, led by unit No. 3052, gleams in the sunshine as it passes a pair of semaphore signals near Purley Oaks sometime in the early 1950s. *Colin Hogg collection/ Bluebell Railway Museum*

After the war, damaged unit 3052 was sent to Metropolitan-Cammell for structural repair and then to the Pullman workshops at Preston Park for internal restoration. In the course of this work, the two motor coaches were marshalled at opposite ends to the unit's pre-war formation. Such was the acute post-war shortage of steel and other supplies that 3052 was not returned to service until September 1947. In the meantime the two available 5 BEL units alternated daily between operating and maintenance spare and at peak times the 5 BEL unit was paired with a 6 PUL unit to provide the necessary capacity.

A Labour government had been returned to power in 1945 with a mandate to nationalise the railway companies as part of a wider strategy to bring passenger and freight transport under State control. From 1st January 1948 the Southern Railway became the Southern Region of British Railways (BR). The Southern's contracts with Frederick Hotels Ltd and Bertram & Company Ltd for station and restaurant car catering were terminated over the next couple of years but the Pullman contract had several years to run so, in the short term, the company was not affected by the Southern's change of ownership. However in 1954 British Railways' parent, the British Transport Commission (BTC), acquired the Ordinary share capital of the Pullman Car Company and with it effective control of the business.

Between 1948 and 1957, one of the three 5 BEL units operated a Sunday round trip to Eastbourne – an echo of the 1908 'Eastbourne Pullman Limited'. The train left Victoria at 10.40am, arrived at Eastbourne at 12.00 noon and returned at 5.45pm. Apart from this, and occasional use on Royal and VIP specials, the three units continued to work essentially the same daily Brighton Belle schedule throughout the 1950s and early 1960s. The three units were refurbished by Pullman in 1955 (3051, 3052) and 1956 (3053) and at some point the troublesome 'Dutch' bogies replaced to improve the ride.

The BTC was abolished in 1962 and British Railways was restructured as a business under the chairmanship of Dr Richard Beeching, with a mandate to return the railways to profitability. Having acquired the preference shares of the Pullman Car Company, BR integrated the business with its hotels and catering services. Perhaps as a result of this change of ownership, BR decided to increase the utilisation of the Brighton Belle fleet by operating an extra daily round trip with effect from the September 1963 timetable change. The new schedule included a late evening post-theatre service that left Victoria at 11.00pm and called additionally at Haywards Heath. The revised schedule had the effect of moving the units' operational base to Brighton and timings became:

9.25am Brighton-Victoria
11.00am Victoria-Brighton
1.25pm Brighton-Victoria (not Sunday)
3.00pm Victoria-Brighton (not Sunday)
5.25pm Brighton-Victoria
7.00pm Victoria-Brighton
8.25pm Brighton-Victoria
11.00pm Victoria-Brighton

The Brighton Belle was suspended for most of the Second World War, the cars being reportedly stored out of use at Epsom for a time. Unit Nos. 3051 and 3053 returned to traffic in May 1946 and often worked in multiple with a 6 PUL unit until No. 3052, which had been badly damaged in 1940, was released from repair. Photographs of the Belle taken in the 1940s are uncommon but here is a shot of the 3.00pm down train passing South Croydon on 6th October 1949 with unit No. 3052 leading. The smoke apparently rising from the sixth coach was probably being generated by a locomotive on an Oxted line train. *Lens of Sutton Association*

The Brighton Pavilion is one of the city's best-known buildings and a magnet for tourists. The pavilions on the Brighton Line are obscure by comparison yet seen fleetingly by thousands of railway passengers every day. There are eight in total, four being located at each end of the superb Ouse Valley viaduct which, as its name implies, takes the railway line across the infant waters of the river Ouse. Here, the 3.00pm *ex*-Victoria, with unit No. 3053 leading, is seen crossing the viaduct on the bright autumn day of 18th September 1957. An arch of one of the pavilions provides the perfect frame for the picture. *John Beckett*

The 3.00pm Victoria to Brighton train, led by unit No. 3051, leaves the Ouse Valley viaduct with a pavilion on the left on 24th October 1965. *John Beckett*

AD 6911/A10   Printed in Gt. Britain at The William Chappell Press, London, E.15 by A White & Co., Ltd.   G6793

Dating from 1961, this brochure shows somewhat stylised Pullman cars apparently heading into the Brighton Pavilion. *Antony Ford Collection*

FROM SEPTEMBER 9

ALL-PULLMAN LUXURY

BRIGHTON BELLES

British Railways
SOUTHERN REGION

AD9667/A25/21863

The extra services in 1963 were advertised with a stylish ('very Hardy Amies fashions') day and night theme. Passengers ('executives and housewives' – the idea of female executives was apparently not considered in 1963) were urged to travel to town on the 9.25am from Brighton and return on the 11.00pm after a West End show. Supper could be enjoyed on the late train stabled at platform 17 from 10.00pm, and inclusive First or Second Class packages including up travel on the 9.25am, 1.25pm or 5.25pm, Pullman supplements and supper on the 11.00pm down, were available. *Antony Ford Collection*

Chapter 11
Belle Performance

Railway operations run to a timetable that ensures the capacity of a particular route is optimised for the traffic it carries and that frequencies and that journey times are commercially attractive. We saw in Chapter 5 how the Southern Railway had extensively upgraded the infrastructure of its Brighton main line to handle both the increased frequency of fast and stopping passenger trains as well as the considerable volume of freight traffic that the railway carried at the time. Even so, the route from London Victoria to Brighton constrained its operators in several ways.

Topographically, the route had presented its builders with a number of engineering problems, in particular, the crossing of the chalk North and South Downs and the High Weald sandstone ridge between Three Bridges and Haywards Heath. Like most lines built in the earlier part of the Nineteenth Century, gradients were fairly modest to enable the relatively underpowered steam locomotives of the 1840s and 1850s to cope. The Downs and the High Weald were dealt with by the boring of substantial tunnels – Merstham for the North Downs, Balcombe for the High Weald and Clayton for the South Downs, with shorter tunnels at Redhill, Haywards Heath and Patcham. In addition, the valley carved by the infant River Ouse is crossed by Rastrick's magnificent Ouse Valley viaduct whilst trains have to heave themselves up Grosvenor Bank on departing Victoria to cross the Thames. The result of all this is that the line is a series of ups and downs, mostly at 1 in 264 (i.e. the line climbs or falls 1 yard for every 264 yards travelled), between East Croydon and Brighton. So, it's up for 8 miles to clear the North Downs at Merstham Tunnel, down for 7 miles to Horley, up for 6½ miles to Balcombe Tunnel then down for 7 miles to a point just before Wivelsfield station. Finally, up for 5½ miles to pierce the South Downs at the south end of Clayton Tunnel and then a last 5 miles downhill into Brighton where the station itself is perched some height above the seafront.

Next, the track layouts must be considered. The Brighton Line has always been extremely busy and, to cope with the ever-increasing traffic, the line was quadrupled between London and the northern entrance of Balcombe Tunnel between 1894 and 1910. The line becomes double track from here to traverse the tunnel and the Ouse Valley, then briefly reverts to four tracks from Copyhold Junction and through Haywards Heath station. The rest of the line is double track until Preston Park.

Speed restricted location: 50mph – Redhill Sand tunnel. *John Scrace*

The 15.00 Victoria-Brighton service headed by unit 3051 approaches Balcombe station on 31st May 1968. *John Scrace*

Upon electrification, signal spacing and sighting distances mandated an overall speed limit of 60mph in the London suburbs, increasing to a maximum of 75mph south of Croydon. Lower limits applied at specific locations such as 45mph for the junctions at Balham, 40mph through East Croydon, 50mph for the divergence of the Quarry Line at Coulsdon North and again at Earlswood where the express tracks converge with the original main line through Redhill.

Then there are the trains themselves. One relevant factor here is the "power to weight ratio" (p:w), which is obtained by dividing the available power by the weight of the train, (in this instance expressed as horsepower per imperial ton). A 10-car 'Brighton Belle' train weighed 498 tons and, with 3600hp available had a p:w ratio of 7.2hp per ton. One 5-car unit on its own weighed half as much and had half the installed power so the p:w ratio was constant – this consistency is one of the advantages of electric multiple units. A 12-car train made up of one each of the Belle's sister pre-war express units, 6 PUL + 6 PAN weighed in at 266 + 244 = 510 tons. These units were mechanically and electrically similar to the Belle motor coaches, with the same 3600hp available (p:w ratio 7.1).

Power and weight are not the only factors to be considered. As a train accelerates, the powerplant (in this case, the traction motors), has to get the unit to the desired speed by overcoming the inertia of the train, the friction ("rolling resistance") of the wheel and motor bearings and drag on the train body as it moves through air. A further factor is the design of the traction electrical equipment and the ratios of the gears through which the motors drive the axles, which represent a trade-off between power on the one hand and starting tractive effort on the other. For the Belle and her sisters, acceleration tailed off

at speeds above 70mph and anything at 75mph or over tended to be gravity assisted – i.e: downhill. Finally the power available to an electric train depends on the supply. 660 volts was available at the feeder substations but this could drop as low as the mid 500s or less in the third rail depending on distance from the supply point and the current drawn by other trains in the vicinity; a nominal 600V was assumed.

Nevertheless the pre-war express fleets were able to achieve the 60 minute schedule with relative ease and, with a clear run, to improve on it substantially. The 50-minute timing originally envisaged by the LBSCR would certainly have been possible but for the volume of other traffic on the route. There was little point in hurtling from Croydon to Hassocks at 75mph only to be met by a succession of yellow and red signals all the rest of the way to Brighton as one caught up the preceding stopping service. In fact, the only time when hard running was required was if the train had been delayed en route and the motorman had to use more power to reach the coast or city within the hour. With the installed power of the BEL units, this was something of a pushover, and, as the Belle services avoided both morning and evening peaks, seriously late running was a rare event. The highest, speeds, if required, were on the downhill, straight stretches between Earlswood and Balcombe Tunnel Junction, then, providing nothing got in the way at Haywards Heath or Keymer Junction, another whiz to Clayton Tunnel.

So higher speeds were just not required and, given the Belle's tendency to rough riding could be rather uncomfortable. In any case, who really wanted to save a few minutes when savouring the opulence and comfort of a trip on the Brighton Belle?

43

Chapter 12
Belle Life

Throughout its independent existence the Pullman Car Company Ltd had been a small but profitable business. Its success was built on consistently high standards of service delivered by a tightly-knit organisation with short lines of communication from top to bottom. Its head office was a modest suite of rooms adjacent to platform 2 at Victoria station, top management knew the key on-board staff personally and the company's inspectors kept an effective grip on day-to-day operations.

A Pullman crew consisted of a conductor who was in overall charge of the service on board the train, a chef for each kitchen and teams of attendants, each under the supervision of a leading attendant. According to Julian Morel, a former Pullman catering manager[5], many of the best Pullman chefs came from the Services where they were accustomed to working in a confined space, were clean, knew how to improvise and were well disciplined. Recruits from hotels, used to large kitchens and to focusing on one job at a time, found the task of single-handedly preparing a large number of meals from a tiny, swaying kitchen extremely demanding and many left after a short time.

The essence of Pullman catering was simple fare, using the best ingredients and served with style. Main meals might include soup or fruit juice followed by Dover sole or steak with French fried potatoes, eggs and bacon or a salad. The meal was rounded off with coffee, cheese and biscuits. Alternatively customers could opt for something lighter – a round of smoked salmon sandwiches with a pot of tea and a toasted teacake, perhaps. Champagne, wine, spirits, cigarettes and cigars were, of course, all on offer.

Presentation was a key element of the Pullman magic. Tables, each with the signature shaded lamp, were laid with crisp, white cloths and gleaming, polished silverware. Meals and snacks were served on good quality crockery by a smartly-dressed attendant (never 'steward' and certainly not 'waiter'!). Before the war, attendants were dressed in a dark blue three-piece uniform with a cap. In the post-war period the jacket was replaced by a white shell-type jacket with blue trimmings. Leading attendants were identified by blue shoulder cords and the conductor by gold cords.

Prior to the 1963 timetable change, one Pullman crew would staff all three Brighton Belle round trips on a normal weekday – there was no changeover part-way through the day. It was hard work, starting with loading and stowing stores. Most of these had been sent up by van from the Pullman depot that backed on to Stewarts Lane depot at Battersea but some, such as fresh milk and bread, had been delivered direct to the platform. Under the watchful eye of the conductor, attendants fitted a fresh, clean antimacassar to the head-rest of each seat before laying up the tables.

As the 11.00am departure time approached, attendants stationed themselves at each door to greet passengers, show them to their seats and charge the Pullman supplement to their fare. Once under way, attendants took orders for morning coffee and light refreshments to be served on the one-hour trip, after which the conductor or a leading attendant wrote out bills and collected cash whilst his team cleared the tables. As the train glided to a halt under the curved roof of Brighton station, the attendants once again manned each door to bid a respectful farewell to their customers.

The kitchens may not have been taxed too hard on this first trip but on the return journey, leaving Brighton at 1.25pm, luncheon would be served and each kitchen would be catering for up to 100 passengers. A quick turn-round at Victoria and a service of afternoon tea on the 3.00pm departure was followed by dinners and suppers on the 5.25pm Up, the 7.00pm Down and the 8.25pm Up. At the end of the day the conductor completed his commissary sheet detailing the food, drink and tobacco sold and placed his order for replenishment stock for the next day.

For all its luxury, the Brighton Belle did have an Achilles' heel. In common with other Southern Railway express units of the 1930s, the bogies were of a new design that had originally been developed by the Dutch National Railways. These 'Dutch' bogies, as they were known, were fitted with an equalising beam – a steel bar that connected the front and rear axle-boxes and was attached by springs to the bogie frames (see illustration on page 36). Although the design had presumably worked well enough in Holland, it proved to be unsuited to life on the Southern and the Brighton Belles were notorious rough-riders. R. W. Kidner, a passenger on the inaugural service on 1st January 1933, describes how these rough-riding

---

5   Morel, J.: 'Pullman'. David & Charles 1983 p148-170

characteristics asserted themselves from the outset – a group of lady madrigal singers, hired to demonstrate how quiet and smooth the new service was, wobbled disconcertingly as the train got into its stride. In 1933, within a few months of entry into service of the Brighton line express units, the Southern Railway made some modifications to the equalising beam bogies in an attempt to improve the ride but without much effect. British Railways replaced them with SR standard bogies in the late 1950s, again with no significant improvement. The ride was lively at any speed above 45mph and wise patrons avoided the soup. A driver gave the following story:

'Recently I was driving the Belle through Copyhold Junction and the jolt was so bad that I slipped off my seat and was left sprawled on the cab floor, however I managed to keep hold of the controller handle to avoid an emergency brake application. Eventually I regained the *status quo* and finished the journey to Brighton without further incident. As I was closing down the cab, there was a knocking on the cab door window. I espied an elderly lady wishing to talk to me and thought, 'Oh dear – a complaint coming for sure'. Imagine my surprise when she thanked me for a splendid journey and presented me with a box of chocolates. I was speechless!'

Below Kitchen of Pullman car 'Doris' pictured at Horsted Keynes in June 2009, showing the cramped conditions under which the chefs had to work. The microwave oven and two-ring hob are, of course, later additions. *Colin Duff*

Bottom The pantry was used to prepare beverages and uncooked snacks and also for storage of crockery, cutlery, glassware and other catering equipment. There was additional storage space in cupboards located in the corridor opposite the pantry. Note the oval window incorporating a fresh-air ventilator. *Colin Duff*

THE BRIGHTON BELLE

Bill of Fare

SNACK SERVICE

Soup of the day with Golden Croutons	1/6
Deep Fried Fillet of Fish Tartare with French Fried Potatoes	8/6
Pan Fried Egg and Grilled Bacon (Single) 4/- Double	8/-
Welsh Rarebit ... 2/9 Buck Rarebit	4/-
Grilled Sirloin Steak with Tomato, French Fried Potatoes and Garden Peas	12/6
Sausages (each) ... 1/2 Bacon (portion)	2/9
Tomatoes on Toast	2/9
Eggs divers styles (each)	1/4
A Pair of Grilled Kippers	3/6
Grilled Chipolata Sausages and Whipped Potatoes	3/6
Cold Collation and Mixed Dressed Salad	8/6

BEVERAGES

Tea	per pot, per person	1/6
Coffee	per pot, per person	2/-
Milk	per glass	1/3
Bovril	per pot, per person	1/8

SANDWICHES (full round)

Assorted Centres (Plain)	2/6
Toasted Bacon Sandwich with pickles	4/-
Double Decker Egg and Bacon Sandwich	5/6

SUNDRIES

Cut Hovis and White Bread and Butter (two rounds)	8d.
Buttered Toast (per round)	9d.
Roll and Curled Butter	9d
Cheeses: (Portion) English Farmhouse 1/3 Continental	1/6
Quality Cake	9d.
Biscuits Sweet (Packet)	6d.
Biscuits Cheese Dry	3d.
Individual Preserves, Jam, Honey, Marmalade	6d.

PLEASE ASK FOR A BILL AND RETAIN IT

In case of difficulty will passengers please see the *Conductor*
or write to
General Manager, British Rail Catering,
14 Bishop's Bridge Road, London, W.2
enclosing your bill.

A touch of class. The vast majority of trains on the Brighton Line were painted in a somewhat uninspiring green livery so it was not surprising that the colourful and eye-catching Brighton Belle had such a high profile. Here the 5.25pm Brighton to Victoria presents an absolutely splendid sight as it heads northwards at Salfords in glorious evening sunshine on 9th April 1964. *J.J.Smith collection/ Bluebell Railway Museum*

The 3.00pm Victoria to Brighton train, which comprises a ten-car formation of coaches with unit No. 3052 leading, rushes through the former Gatwick Racecourse station on 17th March 1956. This station, as its name implies, was originally built to serve the racecourse and opened (for race traffic only) in 1891; perhaps the biggest day in its history occurred in 1918 when the Grand National was held at Gatwick. The racecourse closed in 1940 and the station premises lay dormant for many years until the new Gatwick Airport station was opened on the same site in May 1958. *J.J.Smith collection/Bluebell Railway Museum*

A loss of dignity? Prior to the opening of the repair shop at Selhurst, which carried out heavy lifting of vehicles, the Belle units' running gear was overhauled at Peckham Rye depot and in this remarkable picture an unidentified unit is seen being whisked through Battersea Park station by Maunsell Q Class locomotive No. 30534 on 8th February 1959. This train was officially described as the '1.25pm special freight, Victoria to Peckham Rye' and had a brake van at the rear as the locomotive's vacuum brake was incompatible with the unit's Westinghouse air brake. The unit does not appear to have its shoegear fitted, hence the need for an 'assisting' engine. *J.J.Smith collection/Bluebell Railway Museum*

Satirist Alan Melville wrote about his memories of the Belle in the preface of a small booklet published in 1972 by the Southern Electric Group. The new bogies fitted in the mid-1950s to replace the unsatisfactory Dutch design were themselves giving a less than smooth ride in the latter days of the service, though the track in places was also a major factor. 'Increasingly so in recent years,' he wrote, 'we have spilt a great many cups of coffee, or perhaps glasses of something stronger, down either ourselves or our fellow passengers as she hurtled over those points at Three Bridges.' He went on to remark 'We have also had the most excellent service and courtesy from her stewards. Actors and broadcasters like myself must have learned thousands, perhaps millions of lines while travelling on the Belle to or from rehearsals. Big business has been discussed in these ancient but still most comfortable armchairs. Bookmakers have returned to Brighton on her, complaining of yet another disastrous day while lighting up their cigars and ordering another miniature Scotch'. He spoke about the 'warm satisfying feeling' after a day's work in London of seeing the Belle waiting at Victoria and being 'greeted by a cheerful steward' Seated, he 'looked almost in awe for the thousandth time at those incredible examples of inlay woodwork in the panelling, and regarded with affection the lampshade and the spotless linen on your table'.

Michael Thornton remembers a breakfast incident from 1970 involving Sir Laurence Olivier: 'The usual, dear boy' announced the man opposite me to the hovering steward. No-one needed to enquire about the identity of my table companion. He was instantly recognisable to everyone as the most celebrated actor in the world, Sir Laurence Olivier. 'I'm very sorry, Sir Laurence,' stammered the steward, 'but I'm afraid the kippers are off today'. 'Off!?' The word exploded with such force and menace that the carriage fell silent. 'There are no kippers?' asked the great man, his voice rising histrionically. His arms rose also, in supplication to invisible gods. 'Great heavens! How can this be possible?' We all gazed back in wild surprise as the unmistakable tones that had rung through my childhood, urging 'Cry God for Harry, England and St George, now wrung our emotions beyond endurance over the absence of his cherished kippers from the menu. Sir Laurence's outburst had immediate effect. The Brighton Belle's departure was delayed while a crisis conference took place on the platform. Porters ran panting into view. Trolleys were heaved. As if by magic, a crate of kippers materialised from thin air. 'My darling boy!' cried Olivier, pulling the startled steward into a bear-like embrace and planting a loud, smacking kiss on both his cheeks. The white-coated youth turned slightly pink but showed no other sign of thinking this at all unusual. Some say that BR's intention had been to take kippers off the menu permanently but, whether or not this is the case, they were saved by Olivier, at least for a while.

" BRIGHTON BELLE "

BREAKFAST SERVICE

Cereals : Cornflakes 1/-   Special "K" 1/-   Frosties 1/-
Fruit Juices :   Pineapple 1/6   Tomato 1/6   Orange 1/6

Eggs Styled to Choice (each) 1/4
Grilled Bacon (portion) 2/9
Grilled Frankfurter or Cambridge Sausage (each) 1/2
Grilled Kippers (Single) 1/9   (Pair) 3/6
Hot Buttered Toast (Per Round) 9d.
Dry Toast & Curled Butter (Single) 10d.   (Double) 1/8
Individual Preserves 6d.

Tea per pot 1/6

Coffee per pot 2/-

PLEASE ASK FOR A BILL AND RETAIN IT

In case of difficulty will passengers please see the Conductor
or write to
General Manager, British Rail Catering, 14, Bishop's Bridge Road, London, W.2
enclosing your bill.

The breakfast menu, with the celebrated kippers!
Antony Ford collection

Chapter 13
Special Duties

Brighton Belle units were occasionally used for royal trains and for VIP specials anywhere on the Southern's third rail electrified network, although a steam or electric locomotive and hauled Pullman cars were also used for some of these workings as these trains could be marshalled more flexibly to meet the specific requirements of the occasion.

The working of royal trains required – and still requires today – considerable detailed planning and confidential instructions to all concerned with their operation. The Pullman Company was, of course, deeply involved whenever Pullman cars were used for such services, removing some seats and tables to provide ample room for the royal party, preparing the cars to the highest standards of cleanliness and polish and providing thoughtful extra touches such as bowls of flowers. An appropriate menu would be planned and a Pullman management representative would travel with the train to ensure that the team delivered the on-board service without a hitch.

Unit 3053 conveyed Queen Elizabeth (King George VI's Consort) from London to Brighton on 26th March 1948. The unit was attached to the rear of a 6 PUL unit on the 2.00pm from Victoria and returned as part of a 10 BEL formation on the 5.25pm from Brighton.

The Coronation on 2nd June 1953 generated large volumes of special and VIP traffic, with the Pullman Car Company heavily involved. A party of 300 guests was conveyed from the Metropole Hotel at Brighton on an early (5.05am) 10-car special to Victoria to watch the ceremonial processions, returning from Victoria to Brighton at 7.05pm. This produced the unusual sight of all three Belle units at Victoria at the same time – the third unit had run empty from Streatham Hill to work the regular 7.00pm service to Brighton.

Unit 3052 operated three royal specials in connection with the Coronation Review of the Fleet at Spithead on 15th June 1953. Several members of the Royal Family, including Queen Elizabeth the Queen Mother and Princess Margaret, travelled from Waterloo to Portsmouth Harbour, departing at 12.50pm and arriving at 2.35pm. The Royal party travelled in 'Audrey' and were served luncheon *en route*. The Queen Mother returned to Windsor that evening in unit 3052, leaving Portsmouth Harbour at 6.30pm and arriving at Windsor and Eton Riverside at 8.05pm. The unit promptly returned to Fratton depot (8.35pm–10.20pm) to be prepared for a 9.35am

departure the following day to bring the new Queen and the Duke of Edinburgh to Windsor, returning empty to home territory.

The following year on 14th April 1954, 3052 was again chosen for a royal journey from Waterloo to Portsmouth & Southsea, conveying the young Prince Charles and Princess Anne to board the newly-commissioned Royal Yacht 'Britannia' for a voyage to Tobruk, to be reunited with their parents who were returning from a three-month Royal tour of Australia. According to Julian Morel, Prince Charles was surprised by the absence of a locomotive and enquired whether there was a man at the front. During the journey he and Princess Anne were taken through the train to meet the motorman.

On 13th November 1964 unit 3052 was again the choice for a Royal train from Victoria to Brighton where the Queen visited the campus of the University of Sussex and officially opened the newly completed library building.

Royalty were not the only users of Brighton Belle units for special trips. One notable occasion was the Machine Tool Trades Association's charter of a 10-car Belle formation to take a party of 300 from Victoria to Hove for a gala ball at Brighton's Royal Pavilion on 3rd July 1956. Guests were served a five-course dinner on the outward journey (departing at 8.42pm and arriving at 9.57pm) and a full English breakfast on the return (1.45am–3.05am). Julian Morel recalls that the promoter of the trip, Major Cyril Dennis, had covered every detail, devising the menus, choosing the wines and selecting the programme of music to be played by the Southern Railway Band as passengers boarded the train at Victoria. He even organised a first-aid post, staffed by a doctor and two nurses, in one of the First Class coupés.

Other occasional special workings used Brighton Belle stock. Unilever chartered a unit for a trip from Blackfriars to Eastbourne on 29th November 1956 and again on 19th April 1961 using unit 3051, whilst unit 3053 was used for a special for Associated Electrical Industries from Victoria to Dover Marine on 25th May 1961. Entrepreneur Lionel Burleigh set up a series charter of 5 BEL units each Saturday and Sunday night from 28th March 1964 onwards. The 'Regency Belle' left Victoria at 7.17pm and arrived at Brighton at 8.25pm, with the return journey scheduled to depart at 2.15am and arrive at 3.30am.

In 1953/54 a Brighton Belle unit was used on at least four occasions to convey members of the Royal Family to and from Portsmouth, usually in connection with the review of the fleet, and here unit No. 3052 is seen passing West Byfleet with one of these workings. The headcode suggests that this train is one of the Portsmouth Harbour to Windsor trains that operated on 15th/16th June 1953, both of which were formed of unit No. 3052. The train is running along the up local line while the down local line is out of the picture, served by the other face of the island platform on which the photographer is standing. This unusual arrangement is a legacy of the quadrupling which occurred in 1903. *John Scrace collection*

The publicity for the venture enthused: *Pass under the gay awning, along the red carpet to the 'Regency Belle', the most luxurious train in the world staffed by efficient stewards and six of Britain's most beautiful girls in immaculate Regency costume, who will escort you to your reserved seat in an atmosphere of soft lighting and very quiet Gershwin music. There will be an orchid for every lady, and on the journey down you sip your vintage champagne and relax …*

Upon arrival you will be given a 'V.I.P.' welcome by one of Brighton's celebrated personalities, of whom there are many. A fleet of luxurious cars will then drive you to a first-class hotel where you will partake of a recherché supper in delightful sur- *roundings. After this, dancing, a midnight swim?, or a mild flutter at the gaming tables and then – idle chatter until your carriage arrives at 1.45 a.m. to transport you back to your softly heated luxury train.*

Then the perfect English breakfast will be served as only this Country knows how to cook it. Finnan Haddock, crisp Wiltshire bacon, Sussex eggs, buttered toast and chunky marmalade with tea or coffee. All this and the morning papers too!

However, the idea did not catch on. The Sunday run lasted only a couple of weekends and the Saturday run was cancelled from April 25th due to lack of support.

The perfect start to an office outing? Sometimes large companies chartered a Brighton Belle unit and on 19th April 1961 unit No. 3051 was used on a Unilever charter, and here it is seen bouncing away from Blackfriars *en route* to Eastbourne. The train left the London terminus, which was presumably the nearest to the company's offices, at 12.35pm so doubtless the lucky participants spent the first hour of the journey eating lunch. What a convenient starting time! This must have been a trying day for the SR operating authorities, however, who no doubt kept their fingers crossed that one of the other units did not fail, thus making the timetabled service trains short of stock. *J.J.Smith collection/ Bluebell Railway Museum*

Chapter 14
A Trip to London – 1967

Let us take another trip on the Belle. We spent rather a long time in Brighton after our previous journey as it is now an autumn morning in 1967. Much has changed in the intervening 31 years. The former Southern Railway is now largely the Southern Region of British Railways and the Pullman Car Company is no longer independent, although our now elderly 5 BEL units are still resplendent in their traditional umber and cream Pullman livery, the only change being a bright yellow warning panel under the windows on the cab fronts.

The rush hour has passed as we again make our way to platform 6 for the 09.25 departure to London (public railway timetables now use the 24hr clock). The commuters have all left earlier and the trains arriving convey only a few shoppers and students heading towards Sussex University.

Brighton station, although much the same under its curving roof, has lost its services to Horsham and to the Dyke, while the trains to Victoria via Uckfield, now operated by diesel-electric multiple units, will shortly be history as well. The real change is in the rolling stock. The Belle's original express sisters, the 6 PUL and 6 PAN units, have all gone – scrapped, or reformed into a few 6 COR units to serve out their last days on commuter services, specials and relief trains before they join their siblings at the scrapyard. Most of the distinctive 4 LAV, 2 BIL and 2 HAL units remain, however, mostly on secondary duties.

The express services are now operated by new 4-car units to British Railways' design, coded 4 CIG and 4 BIG. Why CIG and BIG? As with the pre-war 4 COR and 4 BUF units 'C' stood for Corridor and 'B' for Buffet whilst 'IG' was the old LBSCR telegraphic code for Brighton. The semi-fast and slow services are being taken over by the ubiquitous 4 VEP units (Vestibule Electro-Pneumatic, meaning that they had corridors and the standard electrically actuated pneumatic brake) which had already made their debut on Bournemouth line services.

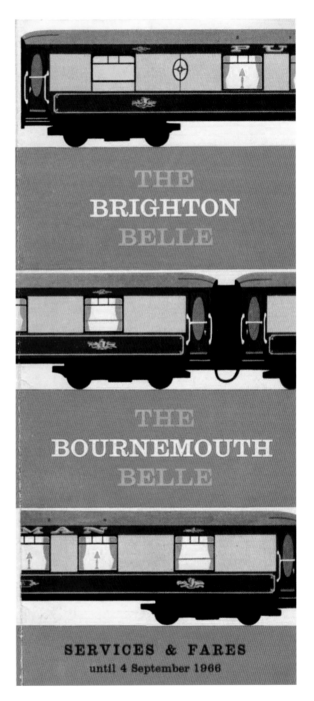

1966 was the last full year in which both the Brighton and Bournemouth Belles operated. The latter was withdrawn, along with the last regular main-line steam services in the UK, on July 9th 1967, leaving just the Golden Arrow and Brighton Belle to continue the Pullman tradition on Southern metals. The artist who designed this brochure was clearly a stickler for accuracy, although 'Mona' (from 5 BEL unit 3053) actually had more equipment below the solebar than depicted in the leaflet. *Antony Ford Collection*

The old and new at Brighton. The Brighton Belle pulls out of the station heading for Victoria as brand new 4 VEP unit No. 7751 approaches on 9th July 1968. The unit was one of a batch introduced to replace the 1932-built 4 LAV stock on Brighton line semi-fast and stopping services. Brighton signal box, which was built in the west wall of the locomotive works, towers above the tracks on the right. *John Scrace*

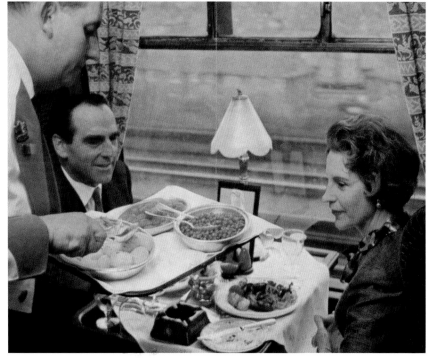

Service on the Belle. Although described as 'snacks' the Bill of Fare included quite substantial meals such as those being served here, despite the comparatively short journey time.

These are something of a design compromise, with high density 5-abreast seating in the second class compared with the pre-war units' deep cushioned comfort but with a through corridor and lavatory access for all. Back on the Belle, as a special treat, we settle into the deep, cushioned seats of a still luxurious First Class carriage to take breakfast.

On our right, Brighton works stands empty. It will soon be demolished to make way for a large car park. Preston Park Pullman works still stands, but Pullman car maintenance was transferred away in 1963. Now empty, it seems to have an exciting future as a railway transport museum and already contains a few historic steam engines, carriages and wagons.

A little faded, but still comfortable. Interior of a motor coach, all of which were Second Class, in June 1966. *Fred Matthews*

Another view at Brighton. Note the trolley laden with mailbags on the opposite platform with a maroon-liveried parcels van waiting. One of the 'hot dog' Brighton totems is also visible. Both mail trains and totems are now just memories. *John Scrace*

The Belle heads into Brighton, passing the Pullman works and a carriage washer on the Lovers' Walk head-shunt. BR's new main line livery, the blue-and-grey scheme seen on the locomotive-hauled stock to the right, will soon adorn (or despoil?) the Belle. *Colour Rail*

We head north, through the Brighton suburbs and the tunnels at Patcham and Clayton, and the country station of Hassocks. In contrast to our last journey, the goods yard at this and nearly all the other stations *en route* to London are either empty or have been replaced by a car park, full of commuters' cars. Road transport, for both passengers and freight, is now the dominant mode in Britain. Nevertheless, despite the modernising ambitions of the BR Design Panel, most of the stations remain in the characteristic green-and-cream Southern Region livery, with each concrete lamp post adorned with a green totem proclaiming the station's identity.

We peruse the breakfast menu. Shall we have kippers? We flash through Haywards Heath, bouncing wildly. A glimpse to the right reveals a branch line diverging away from us through the trees. This was once an electrified line to Horsted Keynes but now only runs to a stone terminal at Ardingly. The branch was once used first to store newly-built electric multiple units for the Kent Coast electrification scheme and later withdrawn loco-hauled coaches, but these have all departed now. We shall meet the electrics again later. Between August 1960 and October 1963, the line provided access to the fledgling Bluebell Line which started passenger operations from Sheffield Park with two locomotives and two redundant coaches. As one of the pioneers of the heritage railway movement, the Bluebell was able to acquire an enviable collection of steam locos and rolling stock and is now one of the world's premier preserved railways. The Ouse Valley viaduct is as magical as ever, but we are distracted by the arrival of coffee and the smell of frying bacon and eggs approaching Balcombe. The train is busy today and we hope we will have time for our meal but as we pass the still busy yards at Three Bridges, a silver platter arrives and breakfast is served.

Above The Belle heads south through Hassocks. It is the closest station to the South Downs on the Brighton Line and is a popular destination for ramblers plus the railhead for the charming village of Ditchling. *Colour Rail*

Haywards Heath. This is a major commuter railhead serving not only the town itself but the neighbouring communities of Lindfield and Cuckfield and settlements along the A272, from Cowfold in the west to Newick and Chailey in the east. Even when the Bluebell line was open, it was always quicker to drive to Haywards Heath and take one of the frequent electric trains arriving in London about 45 minutes later. The goods yard was replaced by a large car park for commuters. Note that the Belle only has 9 cars. One vehicle must have been away for repair during the time this photograph was taken on Sunday 27th August 1967. *John Scrace*

Three Bridges, though, is no longer a country junction surrounded by fields but now part of the rapidly-expanding Crawley New Town, one of the post-war developments that ring London, providing new homes, schools and jobs for those relocating from the city. We are now on the racing ground and, following the major recast of the Southern Region timetable in July 1967, most Victoria to Brighton non-stop services have to do the run in 55 minutes.

Approaching Gatwick, there are major changes. Although the platforms of the 1936 Gatwick Airport station still stand, the footbridge and all buildings have been demolished. The 'Beehive' terminal is still there, but no longer serves air passengers and is overshadowed by a large hangar outside of which sit a variety of helicopters – a mode of transport in its infancy 30 years ago. A roar makes us look upwards as a BAC 1-11 jetliner of British United Airways passes overhead to touch down on Gatwick Airport's lengthened 7000ft runway. We get a quick glimpse of more planes at Gatwick, BAC 1-11s and VC-10s in the colours of British United Airways, de Havilland Comets owned by Dan-Air and a variety of turboprop aircraft, Bristol Britannias, Handley-Page Heralds, and Vickers Viscounts, before passing through the 'new'

Gatwick Airport station opened in 1958 on the site of the former Racecourse station and integrated into the new terminal of what is now London's second airport. To accommodate the increasing number of passengers using the airport, many of the services to and from the Mid-Sussex line attach and detach one of the Bulleid 'tin' 2 HAL units here.

The Belle is flying along now, roaring through Horley, Salfords, Earlswood, along the Quarry line and past Coulsdon. We thread the former covered way at Cane Hill which was uncovered in 1955 and head towards Croydon. The town is virtually unrecognisable from the market town it was 30 years ago. All around us, skyscrapers are rising into the sky, transforming Croydon into a major commercial and business centre. East Croydon station, however, remains reassuringly dingy but is desperately in need of modernisation to deal with its huge commuter traffic.

Below: Seen from the up through platform the Belle heads south through Three Bridges. Many happy hours were spent train-spotting here by one of the authors. The line is reasonably straight and expresses pass at high speed. The passage of the Belle was always the most impressive! *John Scrace*

A whole chapter could be written about the impact of Gatwick Airport on Brighton line services, but, suffice to say, the Belle never called there even for a special working. This 1963 picture shows the complex track-work. Such complexity is both expensive to maintain and would produce a considerable jolt to passing trains. The layout today is much simplified. At the time, there were few scheduled flights from Gatwick and most extra capacity was needed for the numerous charter flights that left for the Spanish Costas and other European destinations as the package holiday boom grew. From 1968, Gatwick had a service every 15 minutes from Victoria with a dedicated hourly non-stop train during the summer operated by a 4 VEP. *John Scrace*

This picture, taken in July 1967, gives a better view of the unelectrified sidings adjacent to the Down Fast. These were often used to stable condemned wagons and electric multiple units. One of the authors remembers two of the short-lived 6 COR units spending months here from late 1968 until their final journey to the scrapyard. Next to the sidings is a very interesting feature. What appears to be a single telegraph wire is, in fact, an early warning system. Should a plane crash on the approach to the runway and break this wire, all the signals will turn to red. There have been a few 'false alarms' when large birds struck the wire, but only one crash has occurred near Gatwick Airport to date. The fields are now covered by the airport's extensive car parks and a plane passes overhead every few minutes. It is worth commenting on the planes that could be seen in 1967. The turboprop aircraft visible to the left of the runway is outside the British United Airways hangar, and is almost certainly a Bristol 175 Britannia. Around 1965, BUA withdrew its Britannias from passenger service and replaced them with BAC 1-11 and VC-10 jets, so this example is likely to be a freighter employed on BUA's Africargo service. At the time, BUA and Dan-Air were the only airlines using Gatwick for year-round scheduled services. *John Scrace*

After sweeping through East Croydon, we part company with the London Bridge route at Windmill Bridge Junction and bear left towards Victoria. The Norwood marshalling yards and Selhurst electric multiple unit (EMU) depot are to our right and as we pass through Selhurst station, we note that the Selhurst Park ground of Crystal Palace football club has now gained large floodlights on pylons. 'The Glaziers' are doing well in the Second Division, and may be in the First Division soon! However, on the higher ground around Crystal Palace, two even taller structures catch our eye. First, at 499ft high is the Croydon transmitter, and a little further to the east is the Crystal Palace transmitter which, at 719ft high, is the tallest structure in Britain. These beam television pictures all over the greater London area, the older Crystal Palace transmitter sending programmes from the BBC, while the Croydon one transmits those from ITV.

Now, less than 15 minutes from London, we finish our breakfast and coffee as the suburbs of south London pass by the windows. In the air, a procession of jetliners from such famous companies as BOAC, BEA, PanAm and TWA head towards Heathrow. On entering Clapham Junction, we are, sadly, no longer distracted by Oliver Bulleid's Pacifics or Robert Riddles' robust Standard steam engines hauling long lines of green carriages towards Dorset and the West Country. The last bastion of regular main line steam, the Bournemouth line, succumbed to electrification in July 1967 and one can now reach Bournemouth in as little as 100 minutes, powered by a 4 REP EMU.

Our bill is paid as we swing over the former LSWR line to Waterloo, past the smoky towers of the monolithic Battersea power station, now with four smoking chimneys since Battersea 'B' came on line in 1953, and glide down Grosvenor bank towards our destination. Main line services to Kent and the Channel Ports of Dover and Folkestone from the 'Chatham side' of Victoria, are now in the hands of the 4 CEP and 4 BEP EMUs some of which were once temporarily stored on the Haywards Heath–Horsted Keynes line. However the 'Golden Arrow' Pullman service from Victoria to Dover Marine, which will leave at 10.30, is now in the capable hands of a powerful 'E5000' (later Class 71) electric locomotive.

There is a complex of junctions and stations around Streatham. The Belle is heading south towards Streatham Common station while the line to London Bridge via Streatham, Tulse Hill and Peckham Rye heads off to the right. The Southern Railway 'Odeon' style signalbox visible above and to the left of the train controls the flying junctions from the Wimbledon/Mitcham Junction–Streatham lines on to the fast and slow Brighton lines. At this time, the second half of the 1960s, these were traversed by mainline services via the Mid-Sussex line from Portsmouth, Bognor Regis and Horsham to Victoria. From 1978, these trains were been diverted to serve Crawley and Gatwick Airport and, arguably, the towns of Dorking and Sutton are less well-served than previously. *John Scrace*

A location favoured by photographers is where the Brighton line passes through Wandsworth Common. The line is flanked on both sides by footpaths and Catsback Bridge crosses the line in the background. A Belle heads south. *John Scrace*

And what are those blue, French-looking carriages with their gold legend *'Compagnie Internationale des Wagons Lits et des Grands Express Européens'* that we see entering Grosvenor Road carriage sheds for servicing? Ah, *mon ami*, that is the rolling stock of the 'Night Ferry' service that arrived from Paris and Brussels an hour or so before us, the carriages and vans having been loaded on to a train ferry for the crossing from Dunkirk to Dover. They will return to the Continent tonight and be in Paris or Brussels by 09.00 tomorrow. The romance of the railways was in the air on that morning. Our journey is over, but the Belle will be heading back to Sussex at 11.00, so the staff are already preparing her for another load of passengers. Shafts of light filter through the cracked glass panes in the high, vaulted roof of the Brighton side of Victoria, still stained with soot and encrusted with pigeon droppings, as we make our way towards the rather less glamorous red or silver trains of the District and Circle Lines from the Underground station.

First Class car 'Audrey' awaits custom. The light footbridge deserves explanation. In May 1962, London's first rail-air terminal was opened at Victoria for British United Airways. This steel and glass building was 15ft above the cab road at the far end of platforms 15-17 and outgoing passengers used the footbridge to reach platforms 11-17 from the terminal. In 1965, 230,000 BUA passengers used the facility. *John Scrace*

Chapter 15
The Blue Belle

As already mentioned, the Pullman Car Company had been acquired by the State-owned British Transport Commission (BTC) in 1954 and ownership of the Pullman business had passed to the British Railways Board when the BTC was abolished in 1962. Pullman ceased to be a separate entity within BR in 1967, after which the Brighton Belle came under the direct control of the Southern Region of British Railways. From 1967 on-board services were provided by British Rail Catering. By this time, the Belle's 1930s-vintage sister fleets had been replaced on the Brighton line by the new CIG/ BIG fleet of express electric multiple units. In the 'Swinging Sixties', and alongside the new fleet, the three 5 BEL units in their traditional Pullman livery looked thoroughly out of date.

However, the 5 BEL units were by no means life-expired. Only one or two of the three units was normally in traffic at any one time and the fleet had been stored for much of the war so cumulative unit mileages were relatively low. The sturdy all-steel cars had been well maintained and did not have serious corrosion problems. The Belle's regular clientele included a considerable number of celebrities such as the actors Dora Bryan, Alan Melville, Dame Flora Robson and Lord Olivier who lived in Brighton and commuted regularly to London and they lobbied hard for the service to be retained. In 1968 British Railways decided to give the three units an overhaul and facelift. The work was carried out at BR's re-fitted former locomotive works at Eastleigh because the Pullman workshops at Preston Park had been closed by BR in 1963.

The Southern Region dropped the Pullman brand name and replaced the traditional umber and cream external livery with BR's new blue and light grey corporate house-style. In place of the former car names or abbreviated numbers, the words 'Brighton Belle' were displayed centrally on the lower bodysides of each car, with BR's double-arrow logo towards the outer ends of the motor coaches and each car's full 3-digit schedule number towards the inner ends. Internally, the seats were re-upholstered in Inter-City 70 moquette – charcoal and

The interior of a second class refurbished vehicle. The common-or-garden blue-and-green check moquette and bright orange curtains may have looked fine on a 4 VEP, but did nothing for the art-deco splendour of the Belle. Most of the marquetry remained. *Fred Matthews*

The charcoal and grey upholstery used in the First Class vehicles was identical to that adorning the First Class seating of the newly-introduced 4 VEP units. The mustard carpets and orange curtains are also visible in this view of 'Doris' (or should we say, Car 282) at Horsted Keynes after preservation. Thankfully, the marquetry and other finishings were left untouched. *Colin Duff*

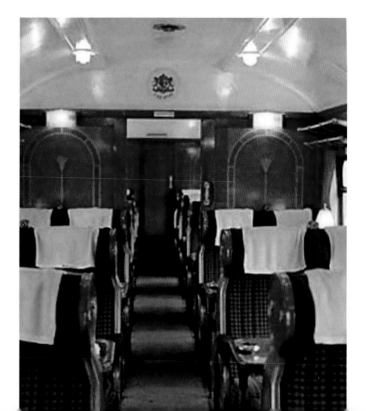

grey (First Class) or blue and green check (Second Class), with mustard carpets, orange curtains and green sun blinds. Mercifully, the original interior panelling and fittings were left largely intact, facilitating later restoration.

Unit 3052 was the first to be outshopped and made its first run in blue and grey livery on 23rd December 1968 on the 09.25 from Brighton, coupled to another unit in the original colours. The other two units were then similarly overhauled; 3051 was completed in February 1969 and 3053 in May of that year. Each of these acquired roller-blind headcode panels in place of the original stencil arrangement and 3052 was similarly modified the following year. All three units were fitted with English Electric motors from the 4 COR pool.

On 12th September 1969 Kitchen First 279 of unit 3051 suffered an electrical fire whilst waiting in Brighton station to form the 09.25 service to Victoria. Much of the damage was done by the Brighton Fire Brigade who used axes to hack away marquetry and ceiling panels to access the smouldering wiring. The unit returned to traffic in January 1970 temporarily with four cars until repairs were completed on the fifth.

In addition to their rostered duties, Brighton Belle units continued to operate occasional specials. These included a trip from Charing Cross to Brighton on 15th November 1969,

from Victoria to Borough Green on 18th July 1970 and from Victoria to Glynde (back from Lewes) on 14th August 1970 for Glyndebourne opera passengers.

However, the reality was that customer support for the Brighton Belle was ebbing away. BR's need for economies was genuine as fewer and fewer people were taking meals on the train, making it harder to justify the large team of on-board staff. As we noted on our 1967 trip, the journey time of most non-stop services from Victoria to Brighton had been reduced from 60 to 55 minutes and whilst this was well within the power capabilities of the elderly units it did accentuate their rough riding problems, especially as passengers were now comparing them to the new standard fleet. The modern livery only made the units look even more out of date and interiors that we now appreciate as art-deco gems then simply looked old fashioned and dowdy. In short, customers increasingly resented paying a premium for an inferior ride on an ageing train with an on-board service that they did not want.

By 1972 the UK economy was in trouble and rail passenger numbers in sharp decline. With the Belle units due for another overhaul, withdrawal was inevitable. The last Brighton Belle services ran on Sunday 30th April 1972, the day before the Southern Region's new summer timetable came into force.

By the late 1960s, illuminated red rectangles incorporated in the roller blinds of the 5 BEL units' motor coaches had replaced the time-honoured oil lamp to indicate the rear of the train, as seen here on a unit leaving Brighton Station for Lovers' Walk depot. *John Scrace*

Summer at Balcombe, as a London-bound Belle is seen through the over-bridge at the country end of the station. Passengers can board 12-car trains at the end of the down platform, but are advised not to enter this very narrow part when expresses are passing! *John Scrace*

The Belle heads down the Quarry line towards Brighton. Although this area looks very rural, the train is near the British Industrial Sand works at Holmethorpe and a sea of light industrial units is on its right. The BIS works has now been swept away and replaced by housing. *John Scrace*

A quiet interlude at platform 16 at Victoria in 1970 as the water tanks are filled. Note the plates hung beside the doors to indicate the cars for those with reserved seats. *Michael Baker*

Supplementary fares of 20p, or 30p to travel in luxury. This fingerboard was displayed in the former museum at Horsted Keynes Station, Bluebell Railway. *Colin Duff*

Chapter 16
Last Rites

With the news that the Belle was to be withdrawn, a number of special workings were arranged for enthusiasts and well-wishers to take a final, nostalgic journey. In these last months of service with British Rail, the three 5 BEL units reached places that had never seen a Pullman, let alone the Brighton Belle! On the 1st April 1972, the Railway Correspondence and Travel Society (RCTS) ran a very complex special with 5 BEL unit 3053. This tour was repeated, along exactly the same routes, the following week (8th April). Departing from Waterloo around 10.00, the RCTS special headed round the Hounslow loop then onwards to Portsmouth Harbour via Chertsey, Woking and Havant. Following reversal at Portsmouth, 3053 headed east to Bognor Regis and Littlehampton, then up the mid-Sussex line via Horsham to Three Bridges. Another reversal took the train to Ore via Lewes and Eastbourne, then steps were retraced to Lewes to allow a trip down the Seaford branch with the obligatory diversion into Newhaven Harbour. Finally, the tour headed for Brighton via Falmer to finish with a fast run back to Victoria (57 minutes) along the Belle's usual route, arriving about 19.20.

One of the RCTS rail tours visits Waterloo. *John Scrace*

Save the Belle! A young protester makes his feelings known at Brighton on 30th April 1972 in front of the SEG tour train. *Clinton Shaw*

Farewell to the
BRIGHTON BELLE

Sunday 30 April 1972

A free black and white print of this picture can be obtained by sending 3p stamp to the Public Relations & Publicity Officer (Dept RWR), British Rail, Southern Region, Waterloo Station, London, SE1.

Southern

An invitation to the funeral. British Rail announces the Belle's last day.

A final day cover to commemorate the Belle's demise with proceeds going to the Southern Railwaymen's Home for Children and Old People, Woking, Surrey. *John Scrace Collection*

John Bradshaw trading as JB Cards produced 500 commemorative phonecards in conjunction with BT and agreement from BR for use of the 150 Years of the Brighton Line logo.

Tray produced to mark the end of the Belle. The text on the tray read: 'Today is the end of an era. The final chapter in an unforgettable episode of railway history. The last run of the Brighton Belle. It's goodbye to Hazel, Doris, Audrey, Vera, Gwen and Mona. And their frilly lamp shades and old world charm . . . . It's a sad day. We will miss them. But one can't survive on nostalgia. Let us remember them fondly but realistically – as ladies in retirement. What of tomorrow? Vast modernisation schemes are already being implemented. New stations are replacing the old. Faster trains are bringing centres closer together. And plans are well advanced to improve facilities not only on trains but stations, and to spread the service until it covers not merely the best in food and drinks, but whatever travellers may need. It's a lot to do, and in the doing of it some once popular services will go the way of the Brighton Belle. Sad – but there it is. We must utilise our resources where they are most needed – to invest in a service for today's traveller. Our intentions are clear. Our aims and ambitions are to give you, the traveller, the finest, most up-to-date service you've ever known.'

Below The scene is East Croydon station at around 14.00 on 24th July 1972 as the 13.01 Brighton Top Yard to Ferme Park freight makes its way northwards behind a BRCW Class 33 Bo-Bo locomotive. Four rather scruffy former Brighton Belle Pullman cars, Nos. 291/2/3 and 279 (the latter out of the picture), are marshalled immediately behind the engine, their faded and stained blue and grey paintwork bearing ample testament to this livery's lack of durability. How strange two motor coaches look coupled back to back. The photographer, who was a professional railwayman at the time, was in the enviable situation of knowing precisely what time the train was booked to pass East Croydon and even the track it would be travelling upon, the latter information being vital to ensure he was in the best position for photography. *Chris Evans*

Opposite The Last Day of the Belle as announced at Victoria station. *John Bradshaw*

Ring out the Belle and let it rest
In some fair haven of the blest.
Dull logic turned aghast aside
From Pullmans for such short a ride,
But here, in shaded lamplight's gleam
The airy fabric of a dream
Sustained by kippers, toast and tea
Could reach the heights of fantasy.
A dragon, legendary beast,
Cropped at the grass at Croydon (East)
And bashful wood nymphs, hard to coax,
Hid in the trees at Purley Oaks.
All this – and more – at low expense;
The supplement was thirty pence.
Anon.

Goodbye Belle! 3051 is seen north of Patcham tunnel on the 'Cheese and Wine' special on 30th April 1972. *John Scrace*

Following reversal at Three Bridges, the SEG special headed down the mid-Sussex line via Horsham, arriving at Littlehampton, where it is seen ready to leave. *Clinton Shaw*

On Sunday 30th April, the final day of regular services, crowds thronged the lineside between London and Brighton to get a last glimpse of this famous train. Four return services were run, plus a 'Cheese and Wine' and late night 'Champagne Special'. On the same day, the Southern Electric Group (SEG) ran another, less complex railtour from Brighton employing unit 3051. As the special awaited departure, units 3052/3 arrived at Brighton at 12.00 on the 11.00 service from Victoria, giving the rare sight of all three BEL units at the same location. The SEG special left Brighton at 12.20 for Three Bridges, reversing there and heading via Horsham to Littlehampton then on to Bognor Regis. After returning to Three Bridges (with an extended photo-stop at Christ's Hospital), it reversed again and took the Newhaven Boat Train route via Keymer Junction and Lewes to Newhaven Harbour, then back via Falmer to arrive at Brighton at 16.47, in time for the 17.45 Belle departure back to London.

After the SEG railtour, 3051 waited at Brighton while 3052/3 headed back to Victoria on the regular 17.45 service train. On arrival at the capital, 3053 worked the 19.00 return to Brighton, 20.45 return to Victoria and 22.00 final service train to Brighton. Meanwhile, 3051 formed a special 'Cheese and Wine' run from Brighton to Victoria where it coupled to 3052 for a historic 'Champagne Special', leaving London at 22.30 and crawling into Brighton at 23.52 to be greeted by the Haywards Heath Silver Band playing 'Auld Lang Syne' and 'Land of Hope and Glory', and hordes of well-wishers. As in life, so in death, the Brighton Belle passed into history on a wave of food and drink, consumed in luxury surroundings!

5 BEL units 3052 and 3053 ran empty to Victoria on 3rd May 1972 for the removal of dry stores and equipment, later returning to Brighton Lovers' Walk depot. 3051 made one more passenger-carrying trip on 9th May in association with that year's Brighton Festival and the following day it too made a round trip to Victoria for stores' removal. The units were then split up and five of the motor coaches (all except 289) were moved to Selhurst depot for the removal of any electrical equipment that could be useful to BR for maintaining its remaining pre-war stock.

Above right: After reversal at Bognor, the SEG special headed for Three Bridges for the second time. An extended photo-stop was taken at Christ's Hospital, with an opportunity for the tour's participants and Pullman attendants to parade in their finery. *Clinton Shaw*

Right: Absolutely the last one – at least for the next 40 years. Unit 3051 heads empty through Balham to Victoria for its final passenger duty on 9th May 1972. *Clinton Shaw*

Chapter 17
The Belle Preserved

As is usual with withdrawn rolling stock, BR offered the Brighton Belle fleet for sale by competitive tender. Normally the bidders were specialist scrap metal dealers but, with the growth of interest in railway history during the 1960s and 1970s, commercial organisations and groups of enthusiasts would also occasionally bid for unusual or historically significant vehicles. Remarkably, all 15 Belle cars were preserved in one form or another and all but one, which was subsequently destroyed by fire, still exist at the time of writing.

At first sight it seems surprising that the railway preservation movement, which had its origins in saving Welsh narrow-gauge lines in the 1950s and had graduated to restoring standard gauge branch railways such as the Bluebell Line, was not more strongly represented among the original bidders for the iconic Brighton Belle cars in 1972. However, these heritage railways were, and largely still are, focused on steam haulage and the work involved in converting a former electric multiple unit car for this purpose is considerable. Vehicle-end gangways and couplings must be adapted or replaced. The Westinghouse air brake system must be stripped out and replaced by vacuum brake equipment. Electric heating must be removed and steam heating pipes and radiators substituted. The 70V lighting circuits have to be re-wired for a 24V electricity supply from an underfloor battery and an axle-driven dynamo with a regulator and through-lighting control.

Back in 1972 there was a plentiful supply of redundant vacuum-braked, steam-heated BR rolling stock and an impoverished preserved railway could buy a complete set of coaches and put it into revenue-earning service for less cost and time than was required to purchase and adapt a single Brighton Belle car. Restoration and adaptation of EMU stock for locomotive haulage can be done – in 1990 the Bluebell Railway's carriage works staff did a beautiful job of restoring and converting one of the Belle's sisters, 'Bertha', a Pullman composite car from one of the Southern's 6 PUL Brighton Line express units – but the task is not for the faint-hearted or the underfunded.

Many of the Brighton Belle cars were originally sold to breweries to be used as pub restaurants, capitalising on the association with Pullman catering. Six of these, Trailer Parlour Thirds 285, 286, 287 and Driving Motor Brake Parlour Thirds 291, 292 and 293 were purchased by Allied Breweries. They

First Class Kitchen car No. 279 'Hazel' at the Black Bull Inn, Moulton, North Yorkshire. *Black Bull Inn*

Driving Motor Brake Parlour Third No. 289 as 'The Derbyshire Belle' motel. *Little Mill Inn*

were briefly moved to Mistley in Essex during August 1972, then to a longer-term stay in a siding at nearby Manningtree, adjacent to the GER main line between London and Norwich. One of the authors remembers seeing them from his regular trips between Norwich and Liverpool Street in 1975 when a student at the University of East Anglia. It certainly made him look twice!

Driving Motor Brake Parlour Third No. 288 went to Truman Breweries and Trailer Kitchen First No. 281 (formerly 'Gwen') to Whitbread. In addition, Trailer Kitchen Firsts 279 ('Hazel'), 283 ('Mona') and Driving Motor Brake Parlour Third No. 289 went to inns in Yorkshire, Cheshire and Derbyshire respectively.

But priorities change rapidly in the pub and restaurant industry and, as early as 1973, some of these cars were being sold or loaned to preserved railways. This process has continued and at the time of writing only two Belle cars, 279 and 289, are still owned by innkeepers.

As commercial enterprises lost interest in their Belle purchases, individual cars would be loaned or sold to a preserved railway then, once the immensity of the task of restoring them became apparent, they were moved on again. Many of the Belle cars have spent considerable periods in open air storage in this way and, because of the consequent deterioration, their subsequent restoration has proved all the more difficult. It looked as though many of the former Brighton Belle cars would fade away gradually as the ravages of time and weather overtook the best efforts of small bands of underfunded volunteers to preserve and restore them.

It was James B. Sherwood, founder and chairman of the Sea Containers group of companies, who pointed the way to a new and brighter future with his £10m project to recreate the legendary Orient Express of the 1920s and 1930s, using meticulously restored vintage rolling stock.

The Orient Express Wagons-Lits service from Paris to Istanbul started operations in the 1880s. When the 12½ mile long Simplon Tunnel through the Alps was opened in 1919 a variant of the service, the 'Simplon-Orient Express' was routed *via* Lausanne, Milan, Verona, Trieste, Belgrade and Sofia. Between the wars the service was a byword for luxury travel, romance and intrigue, first captured in Graham Greene's 1932 novel 'Stamboul Train' and two years later by Agatha Christie's detective story 'Murder on the Orient Express'.

By the 1950s the service was facing stiff competition from airlines but its its aura of glamour and excitement was boosted by Ian Fleming's 1957 novel 'From Russia with Love' and the

Terence Young 1963 film of the same name, in which much of the action takes place on the train. However it was Sidney Lumet's sumptuous 1974 film adaptation of Agatha Christie's novel that most strongly evoked the Orient Express in its heyday. In reality the Orient Express was by that time a pale shadow of its former self, patronised largely by migrant workers, students and backpackers.

The Venice Simplon-Orient Express (VSOE) *train de luxe* service, which commenced in 1982 and is still running successfully today, consists of two elements; a British Pullman train between London Victoria and Folkestone (where passengers transit the Channel Tunnel by coach) and a Wagons-Lits day/sleeping car service onwards from Calais to Paris and Venice. George Mortimer Pullman would certainly have approved!

The British Pullman train is made up of cars from a wide range of sources, including former Brighton Belle First Class kitchen cars 'Audrey', 'Vera' and 'Gwen' and, apart from its VSOE duties, is used for charters and special trains as well as a regular weekly dining trip from Victoria.

The two Venice Simplon-Orient Express trains demonstrate that special train services to popular destinations using meticulously restored iconic luxury rolling stock and with service delivered with professionalism and style can be a commercial proposition.

The Transport Trust, a national charity dedicated the preservation and restoration of Britain's transport heritage, has launched an exciting plan to recreate a fully-operational 5-car Brighton Belle unit.

As he conducted research for his book charting the progress of railway preservation in Britain Denis Dunstone, a Trustee and a member of the Transport Trust's Council, realised that the electric train had received scant attention. He noted that, while a handful of important and well-preserved examples were held by the NRM and London Transport, projects undertaken by private individuals to collect, restore and preserve electric trains had suffered from a shortage of funds and the low priority given to preserving artefacts associated with them. His conclusion was that, unless steps were taken as matter of urgency to highlight the importance of the electric train to Britain's rail heritage, many key elements could end up as scrap. What was needed was a restoration programme that would capture the imagination of a broad swathe of the public and raise the profile – and status – of the electric train.

Dunstone persuaded the Transport Trust that the key to unlocking latent support for electric train preservation was to revive the iconic Brighton Belle and return it to the main line. A project of this scale and vision would act as a catalyst for further electric preservation. The Trust was aware of the location and condition of the Brighton Belle carriages that were scattered around Scotland, Yorkshire, Derbyshire and London. After further research and many conversations with owners, they determined that assembling a train set was feasible.

In January 2009 the 5 BEL Trust was established as an independent charitable trust to acquire and own the carriages, to raise money for their restoration and to operate them as a train. After six months of detailed negotiations and planning, the Brighton Belle project was launched at the National Railway Museum, York, in July 2009 and a special steam train bearing the headboard 'Brighton Belle' and hauled by preserved Gresley A4 Pacific steam locomotive 'Bittern' ran non-stop to London with key figures in rail preservation and members of the public on board.

The 5 BEL Trust has set itself the considerable challenge of making the restored train fit to run on electrified main lines and is working with a specialised engineering consultancy to ensure that the unit will comply with all of the mandatory requirements for operation on the 21st century railway – no light matter for vehicles built in 1932!

Fortunately, the strong, rigid all-steel construction of the 5 BEL cars goes some way towards meeting modern safety standards. However, the original screw couplings between the intermediate Belle cars offer no protection against 'telescoping' – one vehicle crushing the body of another in a collision. The gangways will be retained but the couplings must be replaced by something that meets today's Railway Group Standards, such as a buckeye coupler with override protection, as used by the VSOE fleet. This will render the original buffers redundant, though these distinctive features will be retained in situ if possible.

The original traction motors, switchgear and cab controls were removed for scrap by British Rail so the project will use eight of the rugged, reliable EE507 250hp traction motors that were fitted to post-war SR electric multiple units together with BR Mark VI motor bogies and compatible, type-approved camshaft traction control equipment – a project that will involve grafting a new section on to the existing motor coach underframes. These have come from withdrawn 4 CIG units, 1881 and 1499. In addition, the Trust has recently acquired 4 VOP units 3905/18, primarily for the use of their wheels which have less heavily worn tyres than 1881.

The restored Brighton Belle unit will also have modern 'black box' on-train monitoring equipment, new auxiliary electrical circuitry for normal and emergency lighting, and possibly for catering, and a new air braking system. A secondary door locking system, controlled by the traincrew, is now required for all trains with passenger-operated doors. The VSOE company has developed a safe system of operation for its British Pullman set, which includes ex-Belle cars, and this will be adopted for the project. The restoration is being undertaken by Rampart's Barrow Hill, along with carriages from 'donor' 4 CIG units, 1881 and 1491.

This rebuild perpetuates a fine Southern Railway and Pullman tradition of recycling good secondhand material to make 'new' rolling stock. Much of the Southern's original electric fleet consisted of re-used bodies on new underframes and these bodies were later replaced by new ones on the same frames. The tradition continued into British Railways days right up to 1988, when the 'new' Class 442 Wessex Electrics re-used traction equipment from the original 1967 Bournemouth fleet which had itself made use of rebuilds of older stock. For its part, the Pullman Car Company rebuilt cars as occasion demanded, for example 'Phoenix', now in the VSOE fleet, was constructed in 1952 on the underframe of burnt-out 1927 car 'Rainbow'.

The history of the Belle has come full circle. She never really died, just slept for a short while to awake into her new and diverse roles. If the aspirations of the Trust are met, all those who have admired and loved this most iconic of trains will see and travel on the Old Girl as she returns to mainline service. The heritage transport industry has taken on many difficult, even seemingly-impossible, challenges and succeeded.

Car 88 undergoing bodywork restoration at Rampart's in October 2009. *5 BEL Trust*

Car 88 with restored bodywork poses with 'Doris' at Horsted Keynes on 6th August 2010 during a brief visit to the Bluebell Line. She was then taken by road to Barrow Hill (near Chesterfield) to have 4 CIG motors and running gear fitted and then back to Ramparts at Derby for interior restoration. *Ashley Saunders*

PRESERVED VEHICLES

279 'HAZEL'

Trailer Kitchen First No. 279 from unit 3051 was sold to Audrey and George Pagendam after withdrawal from BR service and went north by rail to Darlington in July 1972, then on by road to her new role as a restaurant at the Black Bull Inn in Moulton, North Yorkshire.

Her owners have since had her refurbished and restored her to a very high standard, reinstating her original Pullman umber and cream livery and name, 'Hazel'. She has become a very special part of the Black Bull, at the time of writing owned by Phillip Barker, and is still doing today what she has always done best – providing a luxurious space for good food to be served.

280 'AUDREY'

Trailer Kitchen First 280 from unit 3052 was bought by Mr David Lowther and moved to the Ashford Steam Centre on the 19th June 1972. Sea Containers Ltd bought the car in 1980, taking her to the Steamtown railway heritage site at Carnforth for restoration, during which time fragments of shrapnel were found still embedded in her marquetry panelling from her 1940 encounter with the Luftwaffe. Superbly restored, 'Audrey' is at the time of writing operating as part of the VSOE's British Pullman train.

Audrey is also a film star! In her Orient Express role she featured in 'Bullseye', a forgettable 1990 comedy produced and directed by Michael Winner, and starring Michael Caine and Roger Moore. The 'Time Out' reviewer summed up the film as "seriously unfunny ... no actor comes out unscathed from this stinker". Audrey awaits another call from her agent...

281 'GWEN'

The original buyer of Trailer Kitchen First 281 from unit 3053 sold her to Whitbread Breweries who restored her original Pullman umber and cream livery and name 'Gwen' to serve as a restaurant at the 'Horseless Carriage Inn' at Chingford Hatch, Essex. The end gangways were removed and the seating changed to 2+1 formation for her pub role.

In 1981, she went to the Colne Valley Railway, Castle Hedingham in Essex with the intention that she would be used as part of their dining train. However the conversion was limited to fitting a vacuum through-pipe rather than full vacuum brakes and she was only occasionally hauled by a locomotive, being principally a static venue for cream teas.

In 1988, VSOE Ltd made the Colne Valley Railway a very good offer; to exchange two locomotive-hauled Pullman cars, Aquila and Car No. 36, for Gwen. Gwen was moved to the VSOE depot at Stewarts Lane, Battersea, where she was fully restored and, in March 1999, she joined Audrey and Vera in the Orient Express British Pullman train.

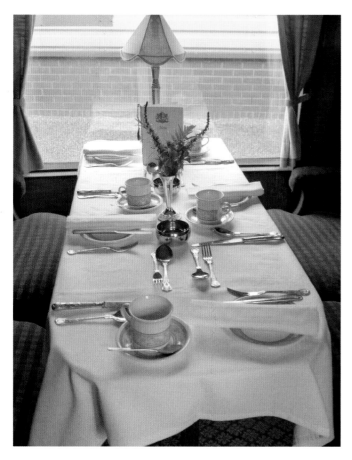

The coupé in 'Doris' as stabled at Horsted Keynes. *Laurel Arnison*

282 'DORIS'

In 1972 BR sold Trailer Kitchen First 282 from unit 3051 to shop-fitting firm City Industrial Limited and she left Brighton on 17th August of that year for Finsbury Park, North London. Early in 1975 she went to Derby for repainting into original umber and cream livery and reinstatement of her name 'Doris', returning to London in June the same year.

For many years, 'Doris' was a familiar sight to travellers on the East Coast Main Line, as she was visible from the platforms on the west side of Finsbury Park station, resplendent in her Pullman livery in the former milk dock. However, during the Christmas 2003 holiday period, she was the victim of a graffiti attack and her appearance subsequently gradually deteriorated.

The committee of the Bluebell Railway Preservation Society agreed to a privately funded project to move 'Doris' to the Bluebell Railway and on 9th April 2006, she left North London for her new home. Her Pullman livery was once again restored and graffiti paint removed from her windows.

The original intention had been to use 'Doris' as a much-needed second kitchen car in the Bluebell Railway's all-Pullman 'Golden Arrow' train but, quite apart from the difficulty and cost of converting an electric multiple unit car for steam haulage, the Bluebell Railway Society recognised that this would permanently alter a vehicle of historic significance.

In February 2011 Jim Kay agreed to sell his Pullman kitchen car 'Carina' to the Bluebell Railway. Built in 1951 for the original 'Golden Arrow', Carina formed part of Sir Winston Churchill's funeral train on 30th January 1965. The Bluebell Railway has taken on the challenge of restoring 'Carina' to her former glory and has released 'Doris' to the 5 BEL Trust, enabling the restored 'Brighton Belle' to be a full 5-car unit.

283 'MONA'

When the Brighton Belle units were disbanded and the individual cars sold in 1972 Trailer Kitchen First 283 was initially moved from Brighton to Slough on 7th July 1972. She was briefly based at Thorpe Park, then at the nearby Eastley End Restaurant before moving in April 1974 to the Brighton Belle Inn (previously the Railway Inn), at Winsford in Cheshire. After 24 years as a restaurant, she was sold to VSOE Ltd in April 1998 and is now stored at Stewarts Lane depot in south London as part of the reserve fleet.

284 'VERA'

Trailer Kitchen First 284 was originally sold to Mr Anedee Turner and was taken by low loader to the large garden of his private residence at Westleton, Suffolk. In 1988 she was sold to VSOE Ltd who carried out a full renovation to their usual superb standard, reinstating her original umber and cream livery and restoring her original name, 'Vera'. She entered service in the VSOE British Pullman set from August 1990 and, in September 1991, Vera and Audrey, with other VSOE Pullman cars, took part in a recreation of the Brighton Belle to celebrate the 150th anniversary of the London to Brighton line.

285

Another of the 'Allied Brewery Six', Trailer Parlour Third no. 285 from unit 3053, spent a short while at Manningtree before being moved to the the Nags Head, Mickleover, Derbyshire for use as a restaurant, where she was restored externally to her original, pre-1968 livery as Car No. 85.

In 1993 Scottish & Newcastle Breweries donated Car No. 85, by this time without internal fittings, to the Severn Valley Railway (SVR) who intended to use her as part of their dining train. This plan was not carried through and, after prolonged storage in the SVR's Arley sidings, she was resold to VSOE Ltd in April 1998 and sent to Stewarts Lane to join its reserve fleet.

However, the VSOE is focusing on First Class cars for its British Pullman train and so regarded Car No. 85 as surplus to its requirements, even attempting to sell the car on the auction website eBay where it failed to reach the reserve price. She has since been acquired by the 5 BEL Trust and is at the time of writing undergoing restoration at Rampart Carriage and Wagon Services in Barrow Hill, near Chesterfield, Derbyshire.

286

Trailer Parlour Third No. 286 was one of the 'Allied Breweries Six' and, after leaving Brighton on the 29th June 1972, spent nearly three years in a siding at Manningtree before moving on to York on the 18th May 1975, then to Steamtown, Carnforth, where restoration was started but not fully completed. 286 was later acquired by VSOE Ltd and joined 'Mona' and other Pullman cars as part of the company's reserve fleet.

287

After leaving Brighton on the 29th June 1972 Trailer Parlour Third No. 287 from unit 3052 was stored at Manningtree, together with Driving Motor Brake Parlour Third No. 291 from the same unit, as members of the 'Allied Brewery Six'. With no immediate requirements for the cars, Allied Breweries leased them to the North Norfolk Railway (NNR) at Sheringham, Norfolk, where they arrived on the 16th March 1975.

Both cars were externally restored to Pullman umber-and-cream livery as Cars 87 and 91 respectively, in the course of which their seats were re-upholstered and the rather awkward fixed middle armrests removed. They were fitted with 240V electricity supplied by a portable generator and used in the NNR's Pullman 'Wine and Dine' trains, although as they retained air brakes, they could only be hauled by a few steam locos.

In John Hadfield's 1959 book, 'Love on a Branch Line' the eccentric Lord Flamborough lives on a steam train on a private railway and a 1994 BBC television series based on the book used 87 and 91 as his home.

In 2002, the NNR leased 87 and 91 to the Keith and Dufftown Railway who found that, due to their weight, they could not be used as originally intended on special-hire dining trains and they saw only occasional static use.

The North Norfolk Railway has assigned ownership of both cars to the 5 BEL Trust and in March 2011 287 moved to Southall for storage prior to restoration.

288

Originally in unit 3051, Driving Motor Brake Third No. 288 was purchased from British Rail by Truman Breweries but, after a period in storage at Clacton, Essex, the company abandoned its plan to use her as a restaurant and she was loaned, then sold, to the Stour Valley Railway, moving to Chappel and Wakes Colne in Essex on 5th July 1975.

However this Southern electric motor coach did not fit in with the railway's GER/LNER style so, under pressure to free up siding space for other preserved vehicles, the company leased 288 to the Southern Steam Trust, based on the Swanage Railway in Dorset. With a view to using her on the 'Purbeck Pullman' service, the Swanage Railway fitted 288 with vacuum brakes, refurbished the interior and repainted her in umber and cream, though 'Pullman' lettering, lining and the traditional 'Car No. 88 Third-class' lettering were never applied.

In August 1988 the VSOE company purchased 288 for its reserve fleet and moved her to its Stewarts Lane depot where she was stored until her acquisition by the 5 BEL Trust to form part of the re-created 5 BEL unit. Her bodywork has been restored and she has been given an external repaint, under which guise she appeared at the Bluebell Railway in August 2010. When work on 291 is complete she will be given a re-engineered underframe and replacement traction equipment. Car 288 is at the time of writing at Barrow Hill.

The Belle on the Orient Express. 'Audrey' visits York in the VSOE British Pullman train on 26th August 1989. *Terry Bye*

Opposite Cars 91 and 88 at Rampart's in October 2009. *5 BEL Trust*

289

Driving Motor Brake Parlour Third No. 289, also from unit 3051, was sold to Mr D. N. Clay and moved from Brighton on the 14th June 1972 by rail to Stockport, continuing by road to her destination, the Little Mill Inn at Rowarth, Cheshire, on the 23rd June 1972. She was "relocated" again in 1974 when county border changes placed Rowarth in Derbyshire.

Once ensconced in her new home, 289 was given a repaint into umber and cream Pullman livery and was later renamed the Derbyshire Belle. She was used as a restaurant until mid-1985 but in 1986 her interior was reconfigured into three en-suite bedrooms, retaining the original wood and brass fittings, and she is now marketed as the 'Derbyshire Belle Motel'.

290

Driving Motor Brake Parlour Third 290 was the unlucky one and the only car of the original 15 no longer with us.

She was initially purchased by British Transport Hotels and left Brighton for restoration as Car 90 at Wolverton Works in Buckinghamshire on the 26th November 1972. Between 1980 and 1990 she was used in passenger service on the Nene Valley Railway based at Wansford, Cambridgeshire, sometimes paired with 3142, the Southern Electric Group's vintage electric multiple unit.

Sold on, she was initially moved to Padiham power station near Burnley where her condition deteriorated. Bill Black and Peter Watkinson bought her in April 1991 and took her to Steamtown in Carnforth in 1991 for a five year project to restore her as a locomotive-hauled Pullman Parlour Brake.

As part of the restoration process, during the afternoon of 18th July that year, hot work was carried out on her and in the early hours of the following morning someone standing on Carnforth station platform saw flames coming from the Steamtown site. By this time she was well ablaze and was gutted before the fire could be put out.

291

Driving Motor Brake Third 291 was the inseparable companion of Trailer Third 287 until water ingress from a deteriorating roof caused her to be moved from the Keith and Dufftown Railway in October 2008 for storage at Holt station on the North Norfolk Railway.

Now under the ownership of the 5 BEL Trust, Car 91 moved in October 2009 to Derby and onwards to Barrow Hill where she was the first of the motor coaches to have comprehensive rebuilding with 'new' motor bogies and traction equipment from withdrawn 4 CIG electric multiple unit 1881.

292 AND 293

Two more of the 'Allied Brewery Six', Driving Motor Brake Parlour Thirds 292 and 293 from unit 3053, were initially stored at Manningtree before being resold to the Brighton Museum of Transport, which was to have been located at the old Pullman Car works at Preston Park and would have seen the two back at their old home. Due to lack of funding, the museum project never got off the ground and the concept was abandoned from mid-1994. Nos. 292 and 293 deteriorated badly and suffered extensive vandalism damage.

Meanwhile, the VSOE thought these cars might be a solution to a longstanding operating problem. Each time the British Pullman set is used, a second locomotive is needed just to move the train a couple of miles between its depot at Stewarts Lane and the platform at Victoria. The company bought 292 and 293 with a view to converting them to driving trailer cars, with staff accommodation and baggage space, so enabling the set to be propelled to and from the depot by a single loco.

On 20th April 2005, both cars set sail for the RSI (formerly Wagons-Lits) workshops in Ostend, Belgium for restoration. Some progress was made with Car 292 – the bodysides were shot blasted and painted in primer but then RSI went out of business and both cars were returned to Stewarts Lane.

Chapter 18
The Other Brighton Line Pullmans

As well as the 15 cars that made up the three 5 BEL units for Brighton Belle services, individual Pullman Kitchen Composite First/Third class cars were formed into 23 other electric multiple units that operated Southern main line services to Brighton, Eastbourne/Hastings and Worthing/Littlehampton. The 23 all-steel Pullman kitchen cars were built by MCWF and were 68ft 9in long, tared 43 tons and had 12 First and 16 Third Class seats. A 20kW dynamotor mounted on the underframe delivered a 110V power supply for the all-electric kitchen. First Class seats were arranged 1+1 and Third Class 2+2 either side of a central aisle and the internal layout was vestibule, 2-bay Third Class saloon, lavatory, 4-seat First Class compartment, 2-bay First Class saloon, pantry, kitchen, vestibule. As with the Belle cars themselves, interiors were sumptuous, ornate and very traditional, with elaborate panelling of hardwood from various parts of the Empire and metalwork finished in 'satin silver'.

Although the cars did, of course, have stock numbers ('schedule' numbers in Pullman parlance) they followed the Pullman practice for First Class cars of displaying names, rather than numbers, prominently on the bodysides. Like the Brighton Belle First Class cars, they carried girls' names that recall the 1930s.

As a result of operating and staffing pressures during the 1939-45 war, Pullman car and other catering services were withdrawn from 22nd May 1942. The Pullman cars were stored and the PUL and CIT units operated as 5 COR. When the Pullman cars were reinstated on 1st May 1946 most of them returned to their original units. Exceptions were 'Olive' to 3002, 'Gwladys' to 3017, 'Ethel' to 3018, 'May' to 3041, 'Ruth' to 3042 and 'Rita' to 3043. In a subsequent exchange 3001 received 'Bertha', and 'Anne' went to 3012. As overhauls of SR and Pullman vehicles rarely coincided there were other temporary changes from time to time.

Sadly, most of these Pullman cars were scrapped when the units in which they were formed were withdrawn in the mid-1960s. However, two were preserved. 'Ruth' is stored as part of the VSOE reserve fleet and 'Bertha' is based at Carnforth at the time of writing.

Of the non-Pullman cars in these units, the two driving

1932 unit No.	1937 unit No.	Trailer Pullman Kitchen Composite
2001	3001	(275) 'Anne'
2002	3002	(256) 'Rita'
2003	3003	(257) 'Grace'
2004	3004	(260) 'Elinor'
2005	3005	(263) 'Ida'
2006	3006	(265) 'Rose'
2007	3007	(266) 'Violet'
2008	3008	(277) 'Lorna'
2009	3009	(271) 'Alice'
2010	3010	(274) 'Daisy'
2011	3011	(276) 'Naomi'
2012	3012	(278) 'Bertha'
2013	3013	(258) 'Brenda'
2014	3014	(259) 'Enid'
2015	3015	(261) 'Joyce'
2016	3016	(262) 'Iris'
2017	3017	(264) 'Ruth'
2018	3018	(267) 'May'
2019	3019	(268) 'Peggy'
2020	3020	(269) 'Clara'
2041	3041	(272) 'Gwladys'
2042	3042	(273) 'Olive'
2043	3043	(270) 'Ethel'

Pullman car 'Alice', originally allocated to 6-PUL unit No.3009, is seen at Ore on 24th April 1966 forming part of the Locomotive Club of Great Britain's 'PUL/PAN Farewell Tour'. By this date 'Alice' was actually running in unit No.3041. Unlike their 'Belle' counterparts, these vehicles were completely self-contained and included First and Third Class accommodation, a kitchen and a lavatory. They were the only electric composite Pullman cars ever built. *Clinton Shaw*

motor cars were all-steel and, like the prototypes described in Chapter 5, were supplied by contractors. Half of the order went to the Birmingham Railway Carriage and Wagon Co. Ltd and half to the Metropolitan-Cammell Carriage Wagon and Finance Co. Ltd. The Southern Railway built the three non-Pullman trailers in each of these units in its own workshops, the steel underframes at Lancing and the wooden-framed, steel-clad bodies at Eastleigh.

Units 2001-2020 seated 72 First and 236 Third (later Second) Class passengers, while units 2041-2043 had 138 First and 120 Third Class seats. A pair of the latter units originally formed the prestige 8.45am and 5.00pm return 'City Limited' service from Brighton to London Bridge whilst the third operated the 8.30am West Worthing to London Bridge, returning as

the rear portion of the 6.04pm service to West Worthing. 2001-2020 were originally classified 6 COR and 2041-2043 6 COR* but they were reclassified 6 PUL and 6 CIT in 1936 and were renumbered 3001-3020 and 3041-3043 respectively in January 1937. Following changing traffic patterns, the three 6 CIT units worked the Brighton, Worthing and recently electrified Eastbourne services, usually paired with a 6 PAN or 6 PUL unit. Units 3041 and 3042 each had one of the two prototype motor coaches described in Chapter 5. It is worth mentioning at this point that in 1947 the number of First Class seats was substantially reduced in units 3041-3043. Units 3041 and 3042 were changed from 138 First and 124 Third to 72 First and 212 Third. Unit 3043 was changed similarly but with four fewer Third Class seats.

These two pages show the First Class saloons of Pullman Composite cars
'Anne', 'Alice' and 'Enid'. *Doug Lindsay Collection*

Bibliography and Sources

Atkinson, J: '5 BEL units' – unpublished paper

Baker, M.H.C. 1993: 'The Southern Electric Story'. Silver Link Publishing

Bell, R: unpublished monographs on the development of the Southern Electric network and fleet

Bonavia, M. 1971: 'The Organisation of British Railways'. Ian Allan Ltd

Bonavia, M. 1981: 'British Rail – The First 25 Years'. David & Charles Ltd

Bonavia, M. 1987: 'The History of the Southern Railway'. Unwin Hyman

Brown, David. 2009: 'Southern Electric Volume 1'. Capital Transport Publishing

Brown, David. 2010: 'Southern Electric Volume 2'. Capital Transport Publishing

Bye, Terry 2010: 'Pullman Cars Preserved 1874-1966': 21st Edition (www.semgonline.com)

Carte, D., Kent, J., Hart, G. 1992: 'Pullman Craftsmen'. Queenspark Books

Dawson, P. 1923: 'Electric Traction on Railways' in 'Railway Mechanical Engineering – a Practical Treatise by Engineering Experts'. Gresham Publishing Co.

Dendy Marshall, C. revised by Kidner, R. 1968: 'A History of the Southern Railway'. Ian Allan Ltd

Fryer, C. 1992: 'British Pullman Trains'. Silver Link

Hamilton Ellis, C. 1960: 'The London Brighton and South Coast Railway'. Ian Allan Ltd

Haresnape, B. 1987: 'Pullman – Travelling in Style'. Ian Allan Ltd

Jenkinson, D. 1990: 'British Railway Carriages of the 20th Century – Volume 2'. Patrick Stephens Ltd

Kidner, R. 1998: 'Pullman Trains in Britain'. Oakwood Press

Lambert, Tim: 'A brief history of Brighton' online at http://www.localhistories.org/brighton.html

Lumley, John: unpublished data on Southern Electric fleets and operations.

Moody, G.T. 1979: 'Southern Electric 1909-1979': 5th Edition. Ian Allan Ltd

Morel, J. 1983: 'Pullman'. David & Charles Ltd

Morris, J. and Ford, A. 2007: 'Pullman Pride'. Noodle Books

'The Southern Way' magazine, edited by Kevin Robertson

Vent, A.P. (editor) 2009: 'Sussex Motorman – The Hubert Hobden Memoirs: Volume Two 1935-1961'. Buggleskelly Books

White, H.P. 1971: 'A Regional History of the Railways of Great Britain: Volume 2 – Southern England'. David & Charles Ltd

Winkworth, D.W. 1988: 'Southern Titled Trains'. David & Charles Ltd

In the mid-1990s the famous name Brighton Belle was revived and bestowed upon the 16.52 Brighton to Victoria and 18.00 return on Sundays only. Here the up train is seen waiting to leave Brighton on 24th September 1995 formed of 4 CIG 1869, 4 BIG 2251 and another 4 CIG, 1867.
John Scrace